My Best Day in Golf

My
Best Day
in Golf

Celebrity Stories
of the
Game They Love

Jonathan Clay
&
Tom Smith

**Andrews McMeel
Publishing**

Kansas City

04 05 06 07   RR4   10 9 8 7 6 5 4 3 2

Library of Congress Cataloging-in-Publication Data

My best day in golf : celebrity stories of the game they love /
 [compiled by] Jonathan Clay with Tom Smith.
   p. cm.
 ISBN 0-7407-3318-4
   1. Golf—Anecdotes. 2. Celebrities—Anecdotes. I. Clay,
 Jonathan. II. Smith, Tom, 1975–
 GV967.M82   2003
 796.352–dc21

                                    2003049786

Book design and composition by
Kelly & Company, Lee's Summit, Missouri

Contents

Acknowledgments

We would like to thank all the participants for taking time out of their busy schedules to regale us with their experiences in and around the great game of golf. If it weren't for their passion for the game this project wouldn't have been possible.

A special thank-you goes to Linda Marino, who transcribed the interviews and made the stories easy to write. We could not have done it without her.

We would like to thank our editor, Patrick Dobson, for his continual support, encouragement, and patience throughout the project.

Thanks to the following people for putting up with our constant persistence to schedule the interviews and approvals: David Abell, Jackie Agnolet, Rosanne Badowski, Kathy Bayer, Sylvie Beauregard, Alan Berger, Suzie Bills, Dave Bober, Buck Branson, Laura Blackann, Jay Burton, Clare Cook, Diane Darsch, Sarah Drew, Laure Dunham, Dusty, Renee Earnest, Sharon Elder, Sandy Farrell, Tina Fields, Tom Frechette, Jason Fox, Doc Giffen, Ward Grant, Jan Greenberg, Michael Hantman, Alan Hendricks, Cathie Hurlburt, Rich Katz, Felicia Farr Lemmon, Toby Mamis, Shannon Meeks, Danny Meyer, Melissa Minker, Laura Minter, Chris Murray, Maureen Radigan, Jason Rafalian, Del Reddy, Scott Sayers, Tim Smith, Cynthia Snyder, Carol Stair, Penny Thompson, and Sarah Werstler.

Jemel Creary, Curt Curtis, Bill Colvin, Bill Jackoboice, Patti Sinclair, Cathy Scherzer, and Anthony Sullivan were very helpful in putting the project together.

My Best Day in Golf

ON THE TEE
BEN CRENSHAW

Ben Crenshaw's second Masters title cemented his place in golf history. The exciting 1995 win occurred one week after the death of his mentor, Harvey Penick, who introduced him to the game at age eight.

I enjoy competing and found at an early age that in golf you were not only competing against yourself, you were competing against nature and others as adversaries. It's an eternal foe, golf is, and you can never put your finger on it. Sometimes you feel good about what you're doing and other days you feel sort of hopeless. That's the nature of golf, it's tremendously humanizing. That's sort of its endless fascination. I've learned from golf every day of my life, and I'll never forget what my old teacher, Harvey Penick, said to me the day before his death. He said, "I learn about golf every day." That's good enough for me.

Playing in the '95 Masters, we were thinking about Harvey the whole week. We knew this was going to happen sometime; he was ninety years old. I couldn't believe that I was receiving this opportunity at my favorite tournament, such an important championship just after his death. To have carried it out was beyond comprehension and an indescribable feeling. I tried not to think about it, but by the last hole, the emotions really started to get to me. I don't know how I stayed together. I knew I could do it [win a Masters] again, but I felt like time wasn't on my side. It's pretty rare when you're past forty that you win a tournament like that, but emotionally, winning it for the memory of that man was unbelievable. It was my best day in golf, because nothing I could do on the golf course will ever equal that. To do something for his memory will always be my shining moment. He was a man who gave us love, nurturing, and a quest for knowledge. All of his pupils loved him.

Something strange happens on the golf course every day. It's an amazing thing, you never know what's going to happen; a ball might ricochet off a tree and go in the hole. I saw a person make a hole in one that way once, and it was a terrible shot. When we play tournament golf, a ball ends up in someone's lap just about every week—it may be a woman's, it may be a man's. I've seen a ball go down a man's sweater. That person has to be removed just for a little bit and you end up dropping the ball where it would have ended up on the ground. In some tournaments, a celebrity would do that and then come up to the person and say, "This looks like a very difficult lie, how am I going to play this gently?"

My all-time hero in the game was Bob Jones. There was never a more literate person. He left us with such fabulous writings. He was so highly educated and he wrote beautifully and gracefully about the game and its emotions. If he wasn't the best golfer that ever lived, then the golfer that handled himself with the most grace and humility was Bob Jones.

Golf history has been very, very colorful, and there's not been a pastime that's been written about more. There have been more books devoted to golf than any other pastime. It's been around five hundred years and it's thought of as nearly a second religion in Scotland. It attracts varied personalities. Even today, we have people coming to golf from completely different backgrounds, because they find golf is a wonderful way to spend time. Even with friends and people who they don't know well; golf allows them to know each other socially.

Obviously, I've been a proponent of the game, but we have wonderful examples of substantial people who have kept the game going over the years, like Arnold Palmer and Jack Nicklaus; former presidents, like [the first] President George Bush. We've had celebrities and actors; they all extolled the virtues of golf and it makes the game something people want to learn. They keep the game moving forward.

The wonderful thing about golf is that after you play a few holes with someone, you know what kind of person you're playing with. Sean Connery is a very tough competitor and he loves golf. You might imagine that since he's a Scot, he's a very serious golfer and very competitive. President Bush, my gosh, he's an eternal optimist, plays very quickly. His father drummed it into him at an early age, I'm sure. He was around golf all of his life. Prescott Bush was on the rules committee at the USGA, and the executive committee.

As a golfer, you must be an optimist. A long time ago it was said, I believe by Walter Hagan, that your most important shot is the next one. You must have hope, and though it is trite to say, golf is like life. You suffer trials and tribulations out there and you have to deal with them. You have times when you perform well and you try and remain humble and when you endure hardship, it's a test of character. It's a constant check on your temper, which I have not controlled as many times as I would have liked.

C. MICHAEL ARMSTRONG

Twelve handicapper Mike Armstrong, before his recent move to Comcast, was the CEO of AT&T for five years. Originally from Detroit, Armstrong studied at Miami University of Ohio and Dartmouth College before embarking on a three-decade career with IBM. Known as a corporate "turnaround king," his motto "Assume Nothing" helped him revive Hughes Electronics and AT&T in the 1990s, and has made him one of the most watched leaders in corporate America.

I started playing golf regularly when I was in my forties and my kids were about to go off to college. Along with spending time with my family, the three hobbies I had wanted to take up were golf, piloting, and riding motorcycles. All three of those things take time. And my wife observed that flying airplanes and riding motorcycles offered physical risks, ones that would leave her in trouble if they didn't work out well, so she blackballed them, although we later compromised on motorcycles. Thus I turned to golf as it fit the best with my family and my career.

The game became a lot more of a central part of my life through my participation in the AT&T Pebble Beach Pro-Am, which was always an exciting event to be a part of. I joined AT&T in late 1997, and didn't realize that the chairman doesn't just host the tournament, he also plays in it. That was quite a shock. I had not played in a serious golf tournament before, and my game wasn't ready for it. At the time I was a 16 handicap, which is really pushing up against the 18-handicap qualification; I was lucky to be just under the cut. But I did get the opportunity to learn what a magnificent event the Pebble Beach tournament is, and my best golf memories come from my involvement with it.

There are three experiences that I would just comment on as my best memories. The first was the first time I teamed up with a professional golfer. It was David Duval. At the Pro-Am, of course, the amateurs tee off thirty or forty yards in front of the pros, and on the first par 5 at Poppy Hills, I hit a drive that was pretty good for me, ending up being close to Duval's ball. So, as I'm talking to my caddie about whether to hit a fairway wood or a long iron to set up my approach shot, I overhear Duval talking to his caddie nearby, and they're talking about the slope of the green. Mind you, we're 270 yards away, and he's talking about how the green breaks. I thought that was just fascinating, and sure enough, he took out a three-wood and knocks it to within twelve feet, then sinks a downhill putt for eagle. I really didn't appreciate the brilliance of professional play until I stood alongside a pro and saw it with my own eyes. So I went over to the other pro, Jim Furyk, and started teasing him a bit about why he wasn't on the green too. And Furyk said, "Well, at this stage, there's Woods and Duval, and the rest of us."

A few years later, in 1999, I had a remarkable experience with Payne Stewart, the year he won the event. Some may remember that Payne was really having a tough time with his game—he hadn't won a PGA Tour event in four years—and it was affecting his attitude and his life. I'll never forget his play on the 18th on the final day, putting an iron shot from about 180 yards out within inches of the pin to win the tournament.

Right before I went on national television to present the check with Jim Nantz for $550,000 I told Payne, "I'm really proud to present this to you. You were a great champion." And he replied, "Mike, you don't know how much this means to me with all I've been going through. This is not just going to change my golf, this is going to change my life." Payne was a very religious guy, and it was obvious he'd done a lot of praying, a lot of soul searching, to reach this point again. Then we went on the air, in front of the world, and Jim Nantz gave a great recap of how everything unfolded, then turned the microphone over to me, I presented Payne with the check, and tears just started flowing down his face, he was so overcome. I was moved by his reaction to how one can throw your whole life into something, struggle and persevere, and then suddenly realize how much that seminal moment can mean. And, of course, it did change Payne's golf and life as he went on to win the U.S. Open later that year, before his tragic accident. I've never forgotten that moment, when Payne realized that his faith and hard work had paid off for him, and his emotional recognition that it had changed his life.

My third memorable golf experience was the last tournament I hosted at Pebble. I knew that my term at AT&T would last about five years, and the 2002 event would be my final year hosting. By that time, I was accustomed to playing in front of the cameras and galleries. I hadn't yet made the cut for the final-day competition. I wanted to play well in my last tournament—but I knew that mid-handicappers like me seldom qualify. I was teamed up with José Maria Olazabal, and we ended the play on Saturday with around a minus-25. I had played pretty well, enough to net us a few points over the course of the first three days, and Olazabal was eight under on his own. He was so consistent, seldom deviating from par, but after we finished I still didn't think we were in the hunt. So I went off to perform some of my host duties when lo and behold, I received a call from the PGA Tour that we had qualified for the Sunday round. This was surely the biggest thrill of my golfing life.

It had a bit more meaning for me that day, because I've had a long history of knee problems from some old football injuries, and in the practice round one of my knees ballooned up and sent me to the local orthopedist right before the tournament started. He took one look at the knee and said, "Oh, boy." He got out a huge needle, drained it, shot it full of cortisone, and gave me anti-inflammatory pills and some painkillers. He then said, "I don't know whether you'll pass the golf test, but you're definitely not going to pass the drug test." But he cleared me to give it a try, and it was a great feeling to call the doctor that night to let him know that "we" had qualified.

I can definitely say that my experience with the game has been a very positive influence on my life off the course. Golf is extraordinary in that almost all other sports are sports of intensity and aggression, and the desire to win can take you a long way. In golf, you have to overcome all those natural instincts and actually control your body to relax, control your instincts not to hurry, control your motivation not to be impatient. Those are all characteristics that in the conduct of business, of course, travel extremely well. There are simple principles that transfer over, like minimizing your downside risk. In business, it's a very important principle to look at the situation in front of you and know that you can't always go for everything. If you're in a position where in your best judgment you need to take your medicine and absorb your mistake, that's a crucial moment to be aware of, rather than try to do something miraculous, which doesn't work in business and usually doesn't work on the golf course, either. In business, often the best things you do in your career are the choices you steer clear of, and that ability to manage risk is important in golf as well. Whether you learn these lessons first in business and apply them to golf or vice versa is probably irrelevant, but it's important they both exist to create the same successful outcome.

MILLER BARBER

Miller Barber, known sometimes by his nickname "Mr. X," is one of golf's great late bloomers. After winning his first PGA Tour event at the age of thirty-two, Barber took ten other titles on Tour during the '60s and '70s. He then proceeded to become a force on the Champions Tour, winning a whopping twenty-four events throughout the '80s. Always a steady money winner on both tours, today Barber spends time with his eight grandchildren and still has a busy golf schedule, where he shoots his age with remarkable regularity.

When I was twelve years old, living in Texas right around the end of World War II, I used to work at my uncle's cafeteria, and I saved a little money here and there. A lot of my friends had started playing golf, so I thought I'd try it, too. I went out and bought a set of golf clubs—in those days that meant an alternating set of irons (three, five, seven, nine), two woods, a putter, and a canvas slack bag. With the war effort going on that was about all you could afford. But that's how I started, just playing with those boys back home, and it kind of got embarrassing for me early on because it seemed like all I did was look for my ball all day in the tall grass.

After that, I saved up for some lessons. When the pro of the Texarkana Country Club, Don Murphy, came back from the service, I approached him and said, "I want to learn this game." To show you how times have changed, Mr. Murphy agreed, and gave me twenty-four lessons at two dollars each. Golf wasn't really organized on the junior level, but when it became clear I had real interest and ability, the president of the country club there in town gave my mother a junior membership for me so that I could play.

When I was in high school, Byron Nelson would come through to get ready for the Masters because his wife was from town. They'd let me out of school early to go and caddie for Mr. Nelson during that week, and he was the first professional outside of Mr. Murphy that I'd ever come in contact with. It was quite a thrill for me—at that time, Byron was the best player in the world, and of course I'd never seen anything like that kind of golf before. It was just an amazing experience. I'd caddie for him, and after he'd practiced all day, we'd go out and play nine holes together. Byron would play me for a dime, so if I did really well, I'd get a dime tip. He'd give me all kinds of strokes, and of course I still never beat him, but he never took my dime either. He taught me the importance of driving the ball. He once told me, "The only time you want to get out of the fairway is when you answer the phone." Byron was absolutely my inspiration to start taking the game very seriously.

After that, it took me a few years before I could really shoot somewhere around par with consistency. I went to the University of Arkansas and played on the team there. This was the old Southwest Conference, and all we had were team matches, going back and forth competing with the other schools. NCAA golf just wasn't a big deal. We had one scholarship divided among four or five of us, and that was it. After graduating, I went into the Air Force for three years during the Korean War, and when I came out, I didn't really have a profession to get into, so several people in the area offered to help me try my hand at professional golf.

The first couple of years I didn't do too well, but a job opening came up in New York, and I took it because that was where all the great teachers were. This was at the Apawamis Club, an assistant pro position. And up in New York I got to know Claude Harmon, Joe Moore, Herman Barron—all the top teachers. Everyone told me that all I really needed to do was refine my game, and so I took a year and worked with them before returning to the Tour.

After serving as Byron Nelson's caddie, it was a huge turning point for me to be invited to the Colonial in Fort Worth, which was quite an honor in those days. I was one of the leading winter tour money winners in those days, but when that came to pass I began to feel for the first time that I belonged on the course with the best in the world.

I think my best day in golf, as far as pure thrills go, would have to be winning my first PGA Tour tournament, the Cajun Classic in 1964. There's no feeling like it in the world. The prize money at the time for the whole tournament was $15,000, and first prize $3,000. Of course, I also got a thousand dollars from the club and ball manufacturers that sponsored me, so it came to $5,000. I thought I was rich—that was a lot of money in those days. I remember playing down in Lafayette, Louisiana, fighting it out with Arnold Palmer and Jack Nicklaus. The Saturday round got rained out, so we played thirty-six on Sunday in almost freezing temperatures. I think I shot 67-65 that last day to win. Of course, I didn't even realize where I stood most of the time, I was just too deep in concentration trying to play my best. Next thing I knew I won the tournament.

Playing in the Ryder Cup was very special as well. It was great to be able to represent your country in international competition. I played on the '69 and '71 teams, but the '69 matches at Royal Birkdale was especially memorable for me. It was the closest Ryder Cup ever. Jack Nicklaus conceded a two-and-a-half-foot putt to Tony Jacklin on the final hole to tie the match, the first time that ever happened in the history of the event. Even though it was a tie, we retained the Cup since we were the defending champions. Sam Snead was our captain, and I thought he was just going to have a hissy fit. But that was just sportsmanship, you know; it wasn't a matter of life or death back then. I just remember having a great time being paired up with Ray Floyd and Lee Trevino and competing against the English players.

Raymond and I played matches against Neil Coles and Brian Huggett on the first day and Coles and Alex Caygill the next. I remember the first day so well. We had agreed in advance that I would play the even numbered holes and Raymond would play the odds. We got to the tee, both of us were stoked up for the match, and Raymond gave me this funny look and said, "Milly, you have to hit the first ball. I don't think I can do it."

And I said, "Raymond, my gosh, that's going to foul up our whole plan of attack here!" But he was getting really emotional, so finally I just had to hit the first ball. And we wound up losing that first day. You just can't tell what's going to happen when you're put into that situation—the band is playing *The Star Spangled Banner* and you realize you're representing your country. It's quite a touching thing. Anyway, we did manage to halve our second match with Coles and Caygill, and I did pretty well in my singles match, winning 7 and 6 against Maurice Bembridge. I was glad to contribute to that team, and the tie with England was really good for the sport, because it was one of those events where literally everyone played so well that it would have been a shame for one side to lose.

Another tournament I'll never forget was playing in the PGA Championship at Laurel Valley. I was in third place going into the last round and I thought I had a chance really to win. In those days we stayed way away from the course because the hotels weren't nearby. This was one of the first times television came into the picture and they influenced the tee times. The night before they told me I'd tee off about 12:15 or 12:30. I got to the course about quarter of 11, and, bam! there was my group walking down the very first hole. Doggone it, I missed my starting time in the PGA. I'll never forget my caddie running to the first tee with my shoes in hand ready to go. Of course, I couldn't get there quick enough. The golf gods preyed on me that day. I guess it wasn't meant to be.

Anyway, the game of golf has been great to me, and those memories are really only a few of the moments that have meant so much to me over the years.

BONNIE BERNSTEIN

CBS Sports reporter Bonnie Bernstein grew up in New Jersey and was an academic All-American in gymnastics at the University of Maryland. She began her career in broadcast journalism as the news and sports director for WXJN-FM in Delaware. She is currently a sideline reporter for CBS Sports' coverage of the NFL and the NCAA men's basketball tournament and also serves as a host for the network's At the Half studio show and the NCAA women's gymnastics championships. Bonnie is known as an engaging and versatile reporter—she has also covered U.S. Open tennis, track and field, and figure skating.

I started playing golf back in the winter of 1997. I was living in Chicago, working for ESPN. I had picked up skiing in recent years, but after several knee surgeries, that wasn't such a great option anymore. A lot of my friends played golf, so I decided to give it a try. I spent hours and hours that winter at an indoor facility right near the United Center, hitting hundreds of balls into the net (okay, check that . . . whiffing on most of them and making contact *occasionally*). I also checked out some of the golf magazines and watched the pros on the PGA Tour to get a sense for a proper swing. I'm proud that I pretty much taught myself how to play, although Jeff Foxx, a PGA pro I've met in the last few years, has definitely given me some great pointers along the way.

I've never really had the chance to play more than ten or fifteen times a year because of my reporting duties. Many of those rounds are scrambles at charity tournaments for athletes, coaches, or good causes, so it's tough to get a true sense of what you're shooting . . . but it's turned out to be a wonderful networking tool for me. Spending time with athletes in a more relaxed setting really allows you to develop a rapport with them, and they're much more approachable than during times of competition. And as far as playing with my friends, it's a great way to spend a sunny summer day. (Yes, I admit it, I'm a fair-weather golfer!)

I haven't been playing long enough to have a big collection of memoirs, but one of my favorite days was this past summer when my friends and I somehow squeezed six people into a foursome. We were playing a course called Twisted Dune near Avalon, New Jersey, and it was just mayhem! We were playing this game called "hawk," where we all take turns being the hawk. Everyone tees off before the hawk and when he sees a drive he likes, he designates that person as his partner for the hole. Because we had two more people in the group than we were supposed to, we were all playing "ready golf" and hitting all over the place. At any one time, I'd look around and there'd be someone behind me, someone to my left on a hill in nasty rough, someone to my right swatting all the sand out of a trap—it was just a circus! I never really understood how the money got divvied up at the end; all I know is the guy who shot the lowest score lost the most money. Go figure. . . .

Another of my favorite moments was this monster drive I hit back in 2000 at the Jimmy V Golf Tournament down in North Carolina. It was an elevated tee, dogleg right, and there was a pretty decent-sized gallery along the left side of the fairway. I was sooooo nervous, because, while there are galleries at this event, they're usually following Michael Jordan or some other prominent athlete, not me! Well, I just mashed this ball *perfectly,* about two hundred yards, which is long for me. Everyone started cheering and I was so psyched, I did a cartwheel on the tee, hopped in my cart, drove down to where all the people were, and high-fived them all! Of course, I practically whiffed with my seven-wood on my next shot, but that's why you have to have a short memory in golf, right?

Occasionally someone asks me whether gymnastics has helped me in learning how to play golf, but I honestly think it's been more of a hindrance than anything else. So much of gymnastics is about power and being straight and rigid, with the exception of your dance. Golf is much more free-flowing; the more relaxed you are, the more fluid your swing is, and the better you hit the ball. You don't need to be strong to be a great golfer (I guess it helps if you want to drive the ball three hundred plus yards like Tiger, though!); you just have to be fundamentally sound.

That's why I'm really looking forward to seeing Annika Sorenstam compete at the Colonial. For her to even be offered an exception, I thought, was a privilege. Will she drive the ball as far as most guys on the Tour? Probably not. But she has conquered the women's Tour, and I'd imagine testing the PGA waters would be a huge challenge. Plus, when you think about it, once your short game comes into play, it's all about touch, so it doesn't make a difference whether you're a man or a woman. I think her fundamentals, in general, will allow her to play well, regardless of the course.

I really believe people show their true colors on the golf course, so it's important that you don't take the game too seriously. Everybody wants to birdie every hole; everybody wants to keep their ball in the fairway. But if it were that easy, we'd all be on the PGA (or LPGA) Tour. Anyone who's been an athlete at any level knows when you get frustrated, it inhibits your ability to focus and perform at your peak level. I guess because I'm a perfectionist, I tend to dwell on things that don't go exactly as I'd like them to, but as I said, golf has taught me the importance of a short memory. You hit a bad shot? You can't do anything to go back and change it, so forget about it, move on, be positive, and focus on what lies ahead. Same goes for broadcasting. As much as we try, no one gets it right all the time. If you make a mistake, make light of it, learn from it, and move forward. As I've gained a better understanding of the fundamentals, I've also really tried to focus on my mental game, which could be the toughest aspect to master in this sport. But at the end of the day, golf has quickly become my favorite hobby, and I'm looking forward to shaving a few strokes off my score every year.

GEORGE BRETT

These days, Hall of Famer George Brett's number-one priority is raising his three children—though he does find the spare time to hone his six handicap on the golf course. Recognized as one of the finest, most intense players of his generation, Brett was a twelve-time All-Star, the 1980 American League MVP (a season in which he hit .390 and flirted with the first .400 season since Ted Williams in 1941), and a member of the 1985 World Champion Kansas City Royals.

I think my greatest day in golf was at Pebble Beach in 1987. I was teamed up with Fred Couples, and we won the Pro-Am, which was a big thrill. I got a chance to play on Sunday—something that Jack Lemmon and some of those other guys would just kill for. Well, not only did we make the cut, we ended up winning the tournament! I remember that day was a typical cool and breezy northern California day, and we were paired with Johnny Bench and Bill Glasson, who are both good guys to play with. On the professional side of the tournament, Fred was in the hunt until Sunday as well, so it was exciting to know that every one of his shots counted. Johnny Miller wound up winning by a single shot over Payne Stewart, thirteen years after his first victory at Pebble, but we were right there in the hunt.

I went out with Gary McCord an awful lot that week at Pebble Beach—we hung out at The General Store, a little restaurant up there on Cannery Row. We'd be there until two or three A.M. every night. Next thing you know I'm in one of the premier groups, playing on TV! And Gary McCord and Ken Venturi were just dogging me, saying stuff on the telecast like: "Well, look at Brett's swing, how can he be a 17 handicap?"

It was the first year they ever did a sudden-death playoff—we came in tied with Wayne Levi and Jackie Lee, the old Houston quarterback. I remember the Pro-Am was just about over, and we were standing behind the 18th green when I heard a couple of officials talking about sudden-death honors and who would hit first. My suggestion of a long-drive contest between Freddy and Wayne Levi didn't go over too big. At that time, Freddy was the longest guy on tour. I thought that would be a fair way to settle it.

On the first hole, I was eight feet away from the hole—I had a 17 handicap back then—and I three-putted for bogey. We tied. Next hole, I'm lying two in the fairway on the par-5, and Fred was kind of tired and a little upset with me after missing an easy putt like that—I had a two-footer on number one. He said: "George, just knock it on the green and two-putt, and we'll win." But I couldn't get it done there, either.

On the third hole, after Fred's first two shots it looked like he was on his way to a bogey, but I drove it right down the middle of the fairway and hit a sand wedge on the green, and he repeated, "George, just two-putt, that's all you have to do." I had a 20-footer and left it about a foot and a half short. On the second putt, the head of my club came back like Zorro writing his name—wobbling in and out, in and out—and I was praying I'd hit it square. Well, finally, I was able to sink it—a par for birdie to win. It was a huge thrill.

Sometimes the pressure at the AT&T can be too much, though. I just get nervous. I'm fine playing with friends at my home course, but it's different when they put up the yellow ropes, the TV cameras are on, and the gallery is watching you. It can be difficult knowing there's someone walking around behind you with your little scoreboard, changing it every time you make a bogey or a birdie. That can be more nerve-wracking than going up there and facing a Goose Gossage fastball or playing in the World Series.

One of my favorite low-pressure events is the one they have the day of the Hall of Fame induction ceremonies at Cooperstown. You tee off at eight in the morning and the only people on the course are Hall of Famers. There's a little prize money involved—very little—and you go out there and play a round with old friends.

The year I was inducted, I played with Robin Yount. They have a pro-am the day before that you play with sponsors and friends of the Hall of Fame. This past year, I played with Pirates owner Kevin McClatchy and Bob Gibson. They just throw guys together, and you go out and have a wonderful morning of golf. Two years ago I played in a threesome with Carlton Fisk and Rollie Fingers. That's a fun, fun day to be a member of such a select group of people. And the crowds are pretty big. They don't let the people on the golf course, but you have to cross the street on one occasion, and they're lined up down the street, all the kids and autograph seekers and baseball fans. It's a great time.

But I think my ultimate round of golf would involve playing Augusta National with Fred Couples, Greg Norman, and Payne Stewart. I haven't played with Fred in a long time, but since that weekend at Pebble he's at the top of the list. I played with Greg Norman years ago when he first came over to play in the U.S. Tour, at the Howard Cosell Invitational, which is the day before the Bob Hope starts in Palm Springs. I remember asking Fred Couples: "Who's this Greg Norman guy? I've never heard of him." And he said: "Oh, he's this young guy from Australia. He's a pretty good player." Turned out to be one hell of a player! I think it's great to see him attack the course the way he does. And Payne Stewart, well, I'm happy that I got a chance to meet him and wish that I could play with him again. He was a great golfer and an even better person.

PRESIDENT GEORGE H. W. BUSH

The forty-first president was well-known for his lightning-fast rounds of golf at Kennebunkport during his time in office. Today, he enjoys the game more than ever, but now his son George W. has turned the tables, as he's the one who can't often spare the time for a friendly father-son match. The Bush family has a strong golf lineage to match the political one: Prescott Bush, a U.S. senator from 1952 to 1963, was also president of the U.S. Golf Association.

Speed may be the *only* thing I'm known for on the golf course. At times, I've played so fast that a good golfer, if he were playing seriously, wouldn't like the pace. When I was president, of course, everyone fell in line. They figured I was a busy man, so we had to play faster, and there was no discussion about it. I just think the game is too slow. On an average public course, it takes you over four hours to go around and that's just ridiculous. There's nothing worse than a lousy golfer standing there, lining up his putt on the green like he's playing for $500,000 at the Open. It's obscene. So what I hope is that by playing fast, and by being known as a player who does this while still following the etiquette of the game, that I can make a modest contribution to speeding the game up. Some pros, including Arnold Palmer, have told me I've done that.

My father, Prescott Bush, was a fabulous golfer. He had a wonderful touch and he hit it a long way. He was the one who instilled the value of fast play in me, and in my son as well. In fact, he once told George W., "Son, looking at your swing, you're probably not going to be a great golfer, so make sure you play fast." The rest of America should have listened to him! We actually used to call it aerobic golf. One of the fastest rounds I remember was eighteen holes in slightly under two hours in Kennebunkport. Of course, we had the unfair advantage of having Secret Service agents sweeping the course.

I'm occasionally asked if the Secret Service protection distracts me from the game. Just as with other aspects of life, the answer is no. They're like having your sons around, except more dignified and attentive to their duty. Now, the security is far less intense than when I was president, but I can say that they never inhibited the game. A lot of them are avid golfers themselves. When we get out on a big name-dropping match with Couples or Arnold Palmer or whomever, the Secret Service men are just as thrilled as I am to be out there with somebody who is clearly so great.

Since I've been playing the game for such a long time, my golf memories have blurred together somewhat. My best day in golf could be a fairway shot from one year, a long putt from another, or sharing jokes with friends in yet another. I do, however, have one not so good memory—a few years ago, I decked a woman named Mrs. Burley during the Bob Hope Tournament. It was after I was out of office and I hit her right in the head. My tee shot hit a tree on the edge of the fairway and the ball bounced off it and decked her. I got up there and her glasses had been shattered by my shot and she was oozing blood. Surprisingly enough, she was very pleasant about it. I didn't quite know whether I should play or wait for a helicopter to come pick her up, but we comforted her and she was very nice. I called her later and sent her some golf balls and a couple of presidential pins. I was trying to be really apologetic, but she wouldn't hear of it. Apparently, I'd made her the most popular person at her club. Her answering machine couldn't hold all the phone calls she was getting.

I've met a lot of terrific people like Mrs. Burley around the game of golf. My family and I have always enjoyed going to the Ryder Cup and talking to the players before the final round. It's a great thrill, going over and trying to pump them up a little bit. I get just as excited meeting them as they do meeting me. Some of the star players have become friends and fit right into our family.

One of the things I've learned from golf is that it teaches you never to exaggerate. That's one of the game's great lessons. Golf challenges your integrity. The old adage that "If you cheat at golf, you'll cheat at life," is something I firmly believe in. Golf tests your inner fiber and your character. That's what I love about it. I get ample opportunity to overcome adversity, since I get plenty of it on each one of the eighteen holes. I've learned not to take myself too seriously on the golf course. I just love to be outside and it gets you outdoors with a chance to have fun and share precious moments with friends.

BILLY CASPER

PGA Hall of Famer Billy Casper ranks sixth all time with fifty-one PGA Tour titles, including three majors—the '59 and '66 U.S. Opens, and the '70 Masters. He also won the prestigious Vardon Trophy, given to the golfer with the lowest season scoring average, five times. Famed for his deadly putting skills, Casper's Vardon trophies prove the all-around quality of his game. Though he started out at a time when there wasn't much money in golf, he was the second player, after Arnold Palmer, to reach $1 million in career earnings. Today, Casper plays in Champions Tour events and works on golf course design on the side.

My dad started me out in golf when I was four and a half, out in the cow pastures of New Mexico. But my real first love was baseball—I thought I was going to be a professional baseball player someday. Then after we moved to California, I started caddying at San Diego Country Club when I was a teenager, and eventually had to make the choice between baseball and golf. Fortunately, I made the right choice.

When I was a kid, I was too lazy to spend a lot of time on the practice tee hitting balls—I wanted to get on the course. But when I did spend time practicing, it was with my short game, putting and chipping and sand play. I remember we'd play cards in the caddie tent until nightfall, and then we'd take off and go home. We'd always stop at the 15th or 16th green to putt in the dark, and that's really how I developed my putting touch. I learned how to putt blind, basically. I would find the hole, form a mental image of where it was, then walk back to my ball and stroke the putt. And it turned out that that kind of practice would serve me very well in the future, though I didn't think much of it at the time. The most important thing in putting is reading the green. I believe all amateur golfers should spend most of their practice time on short putts—those from five feet and in—because those are the putts you're faced with most of the time.

Like I said, I was lazy with the full swing. It wasn't until I reached the Tour that I developed a good golf swing, where I was in total control of what I was doing.

I turned professional in April of 1954, and I played in sectional tournaments in and around Southern California for fourteen months before I joined the Tour. I had a friend who had been in the Navy with me who found two businessmen to sponsor me on the Tour. My first tournament was in Portland, Oregon, in 1955. It was the Western Open, and I won $33.33. You've got to start somewhere, and I started with that little check. My first couple of years on the Tour, I remember I used to travel in a house trailer with about half a dozen other players—Doug Ford, Gene Littler, and Buster Reed were among them. We were very close to each other, looked out for each other, and our wives were very close as well. If one of the guys was winning the tournament, the other wives would watch their children and it enabled the wife to go out and watch her husband play. We had a lot of fun in those early days.

Ben Hogan was always my idol, along with Sam Snead and Byron Nelson, and I really grew into my game watching and learning from them. I'll always remember the first time I met Hogan, at the Colonial Golf Club in Fort Worth. I had been scared to death of him for some time, but I saw him that day coming down the hallway from the pro shop to the locker room and I finally said, "Good morning, Mr. Hogan." And he said good morning to me, in his abrupt way.

"You're Billy Casper, aren't you?"

"Yes sir, Mr. Hogan."

"You're playing some mighty fine golf."

It felt great to know that he had been watching my game, gauging my abilities a little bit, and gradually we got to be great friends. The first time I played with him was at the old Round Robin tournament outside New York City along with Fred Hawkins and Dow Finsterwald. After we'd finished the first round, Hogan said to and me, "You know, if you two guys couldn't putt, I'd be buying hot dogs from you on the 10th tee."

The next morning, when I arrived at the course, Hogan was alone in the locker room. When he saw me, he pulled me over and he asked me how I putted. He asked for a putting lesson. I was stunned, the great Ben Hogan asking for advice. I gave him some tips, and that really cemented our friendship. He gave me an open invitation to have lunch with him any time I was passing through Fort Worth. That was a real honor, because very few people shared his table at Colonial.

My three major championships are absolutely my best days in golf. It's impossible for me to choose between them, so I won't even try. I have fond memories of each of them. The '59 Open at Winged Foot, of course, I won by a shot over Bob Rosburg. I had 114 putts in 72 holes during that tournament, and I one-putted 31 holes. The funny thing was that I used an experimental mallet-shaped putter I had never used before. I remember the late Jack Murphy, the San Diego sports editor, was covering the tournament. After the second round I had taken the lead, and as I was walking with him I said, "You know, Jack, I can always say I led the Open for one round." He changed the subject. The next day I shot 69, and said to Murphy, "Now I can say I led for two rounds." And he changed the subject again. I shot 74 in the final round to win by a single stroke. I won the tournament in the last four holes of the third round and the first five of the final round—I one-putted nine straight holes over that stretch.

In '66 I made the best comeback of my career at Olympic Club in San Francisco. I came from seven shots back on the last nine holes to catch Arnold Palmer, before beating him by four in the eighteen-hole playoff. I decided as we went to the back nine I was going to put on a charge, make pars and birdies. And as it turned out, I made six pars and three birdies, so I was up in 36 and back in 32 for 68, and Arnold was out in 32 and back in 39 for 71. By 16, being only three back, I had the sense that I had a chance to win the tournament. My goal when I started was to win the Open. And once I won it, I wanted to win it again, and it happened to work out.

The Masters in 1970 was really the icing on the cake, winning over Gene Littler in the playoff. This was the last eighteen-hole playoff before they went to sudden death in 1976. I remember I birdied the 1st hole in the playoff and went one shot ahead, and on the 2nd hole I hit a terrible drive off a pine tree. I was in an area that they had planed off, it was a water hazard, but there was no water in it. The gallery had tamped the grass down, and my ball actually had a fairly clean lie. But behind it about an inch or so was a big branch that covered about half the ball, and I had to take the club so that I could fit it over the branch, under the ball, and then hit the ball straight up in the air for about 120 yards to get it back to the fairway, which was the only shot I had. I hit it absolutely dead perfect and got it back to the fairway. Gene chili-dipped his third shot into the bunker, and when we finished the hole, he'd made six and I'd made five, which really set the tone for the round. I picked up seven shots, and it looked like I was going to run away, but then I played 12 through 15 two over par while he played it two under, and I was only three shots ahead with three holes to play, and I thought about how Palmer had the same lead on me back in '66, but I managed to close it out with birdies on two of the last three holes.

I've always been extremely proud of that win, playing against Gene, who's a great friend. I often played practice rounds with him and Bill Kerr and Cliff Roberts, the chairman of Augusta National. They were all great friends of mine. When I finished that final round in 1970, Mr. Roberts was standing behind the green, and he shook my hand. He didn't say congratulations, he said, "Thank you." Evidently, he had been privately rooting for me to win the tournament for a number of years and when I finally achieved it, the way he expressed himself was something that I'll never forget.

I think the thing that I've learned about the game over the years is that you have to exercise a great deal of discipline when you play, and have full control over yourself at all times on the golf course. Most of the time, I would not pay any attention to the score boards because I felt that if I was close to the lead, if I went out and I was making good decisions and striking the ball well and holing a few putts, that I had a great chance to win the tournament, so I really didn't want to know what anybody else was doing because I couldn't change that. That attitude sort of carried over in my life, in being committed to my family and doing what I had to do to take care of them and take care of my professional commitments as well.

FRANK CHIRKINIAN

Frank Chirkinian was the executive golf producer at CBS Sports for forty-one years. He produced every Masters broadcast from the first one ever televised, in 1959, until his retirement in 1996. He was a pioneer whose innovations at the Masters included the over- and underpar method of scoring. His skill at presenting the narrative of golf tournaments is widely recognized as being a major factor in the explosion of golf's popularity. During his career, Chirkinian won four Emmy awards and was awarded the Lifetime Journalism Award by the Golf Writers of America Association in 1996.

I started playing golf in 1954, with Jack Whitaker and John Facenda, who was the voice of the NFL—remember that wonderful voice? Facenda was also the premier newscaster in the Philadelphia market, and I was just getting started, working at a CBS affiliate, WCAU, at the time. We used to play at Llanark Country Club, which is where I televised my first tournament: the PGA Championship, when they went from match to medal play for the first time. Dow Finsterwald won that year.

In the mid-fifties I was summoned to CBS Sports in New York. I kind of went up there kicking and screaming, because I was a studio director, and the idea of being a golf or a sports director, that kind of a tag, did not sit well with me. It was something that I never really got comfortable with in my entire career, to be honest. I go to sporting events only because I'm going to televise them; I don't go there as a spectator. Being a fan is not really my aesthetic.

But that's not to say I didn't enjoy the position I was in, and of course I got caught up in the drama. There are two tournaments that stand out in my mind, both of them won by Jack Nicklaus. I still remember the wonderful dialogue between Ben Wright and Henry Longhurst during the 1975 Masters, when Nicklaus, Tom Weiskopf, and Johnny Miller were all tied for the lead at one point. In the final round Weiskopf made his putt at 15 to go into the lead by one over Nicklaus. Jack was standing on the 16th green waiting for Tom Watson to replay a shot because he had put his original ball in the water. And when Weiskopf made his birdie at 15, the physical proximity between the two holes was such that it was like Jack was standing at the 15th watching it happen. I cut back and got a reaction shot of Jack over the roar of the crowd, and Ben Wright said: "Terrible music for Mr. Nicklaus's ears."

Then Weiskopf reached the 16th tee just in time to watch Jack make that great putt up the hill from 40 feet. It was the first time I'd seen such emotion from the stoic Nicklaus, running off the green with his putter raised defiantly over his head. Again, the crowd roared, and Henry Longhurst quietly said: "My, my, my. Never before have I seen such a thing." I cut back to a reaction shot of Weiskopf, and Henry said over the shot: "And now Mr. Weiskopf must take it, just as he dished it out." It was wonderful, wonderful dialogue. I always valued that more than playing up the athleticism of the golfers, because, as Shakespeare said, *the play's the thing*. And the golf course is this magnificent stage, and the players are the actors. It's always been theater for me.

The '86 Masters was also a great pleasure to cover, the highlight being when Nicklaus made that marvelous putt at 17 to go into the lead and eventually win his sixth green jacket. But even more than the sights, the *sounds* of that year were something special. Jack's iron play was beautiful—just the sound of the club meeting the ball every time he hit an iron was so crisp and clean that you knew it was a great shot. The fact that there were so many incredible sounds that year reinforced one of my long-standing precepts about broadcasting. When you are watching and listening to this kind of drama unfold, whisper quietly, let the moment carry the day. Superfluous dialogue can only kill a dramatically loaded scene.

As for my own best day in golf, it came in 1985, playing at Augusta National with Hord Hardin, who was then the club chairman. We were on the back nine, and I birdied 11 and 12. We were on the 13th fairway, and here comes Bernhard Langer with a wheel. He was measuring off the course—the tournament was only a week or two away. Now, Hord was an extremely fast player—with him it wasn't the score you shot, but how long it took you. He was sort of like George Bush the Elder in that respect. So we waved Bernhard through, he thanked us, and we hit our lay-up shots in front of the creek. He was up on the green and he's putting from all different angles, putting five or six different balls. Hord got really upset and gave him one of those loud, high-pitched whistles, as if to say: *Get off the green.* Finally, Langer got the message, and I pitched my ball up from about 110 yards, then made my 15-footer. And Hord looks at me and says, "Well, I'll be damned, you just birdied Amen Corner." Up until that point I hadn't even been thinking about it. Of course, Langer also won the Masters that year, so maybe his presence on the green that day brought me some good luck.

In addition to my best days, I had a bad day that turned into a good day. It was the Thursday round of the 1997 Pebble Beach AT&T Tournament. We were playing at Poppy Hills, which I dubbed Sloppy Hills after we had finished because it took us six and a half hours to play and the course was under water. My partner that day was John Cook, and we were paired with David Duval and a doctor from Jacksonville. I was so tired by the time I got in, I promised myself, I took the vow: Never play again. And I haven't been back since.

On the other hand, sometimes a washout can be a blessing in disguise. In '96, my last year at CBS, the other AT&T courses were completely inundated with water, so I put together a last-minute scramble with the celebrities. I got AT&T to put up $50,000 for the players to donate to their favorite charities.

And we had a ball—it was a hell of a show. We got a bigger rating with that show than we would with a normal Saturday live telecast. Andy Garcia and Kevin Costner ended up winning it on the last hole. That accidental shoot-out was also the genesis of what I'm doing now—I'm producing a celebrity shoot-out for Gaylord Entertainment, with Michael Douglas as the host.

I've scored a hole in one eight times as well, but honestly, every day I tee up is my best day on the golf course. There's a sense of peace and tranquility out there that I just absolutely adore. I love to go out and play golf and have fun, and there's no better way to learn about someone's personality than to play a round of golf with him. I think golf has a great way of exposing one's character, and I've always felt very nice when I walk off a course and slap a guy's back and shake his hand and say: Hey, I really enjoyed spending the day with you. As opposed to saying to yourself: I don't think I want to go near this guy ever again. I've run across those guys now and again, but for the most part it's always just a fun day, and that kind of camaraderie you can't find in a bar.

I've had nothing but a joyous time around the game of golf, as my vocation and avocation turned out to be the same thing. And some of the nicest people I've ever met have been on golf courses. Now, how good is that?

ROGER CLEMENS

New York Yankees pitching ace Roger Clemens, a lock for the Hall of Fame, would just as soon talk about golf as his six Cy Young awards. He has picked up more tales in seventeen years of golfing than a lot of duffers collect in a lifetime, including once allowing a tornado to play through during a Houston-area tournament in 1988.

We actually saw the tornado touch down. I'll never forget how fast it hit, it was one scary moment. It took me off my feet, wrecked the clubhouse, and turned over a car. It was devastating.

I started playing professional baseball in 1984. I got my first set of clubs from my wife, Debbie, at the end of the '86 season and started playing then. Within six months of picking up the game and not even being able to get the ball airborne half the time, I'd gotten myself down to a 16 handicap; now I'm a six. Golf has taught me more patience. Being a power pitcher, I'm challenging hitters and myself constantly, and that's what's great about golf. There are challenges I have been able to accomplish in baseball, but there are still some things I want to work on. Golf teaches you that patience.

My best day in golf? Well, I've had three holes in one and the first one was really memorable, because it was my first and it came right after the birth of our second son, Kory, in May 1988.

Actually, I wasn't even supposed to be on the golf course. Debbie was in labor and I left the Red Sox in Anaheim and flew home to Houston. The following day, she gave birth. The next morning, I went to pass out cigars at the country club, and my brother-in-law and a friend were out there. The next thing you know, they talked me into getting out on the 1st tee.

I was supposed to bring lunch back to the hospital by two o'clock, so I figured, no problem, it was ten. So I'm out there to play a couple of holes. I'm on the tee for the par-3 2nd hole and I drained it. Now they're telling me you've got to finish the round or it doesn't count. Since I'm away from the team, I'm not supposed to be playing, but by the time we make the turn, the pro and everybody in the clubhouse knows. I told them to put it in the back part of the paper, because I didn't want this making any kind of news at all.

The next day it was in *USA Today*! I figured I'd have to talk my way out of it back at the hospital, so I brought half the people at the golf course with me as witnesses. My wife wouldn't hear me out. At first, she had a pretty nasty look on her face, but when I dropped it on her that I made my first hole in one, she got pretty excited. I always tell Kory that if he weren't born, I never would have had a hole in one.

One moment I still laugh about is playing golf with Jose Canseco for the first time. He'd been bugging me about playing for a few years. He came to Boston in 1995 and I knew he hadn't played too much, but I'll play with anybody.

We go to The Country Club in Brookline, just down the road from Fenway. They like guests on the course early, like at seven A.M., so we don't get in the way of any of the members. So he's supposed to meet me there at seven A.M. sharp. That morning, it's a warm June day. I'm out there with two other guys and there are a couple of members smoking cigars and hitting a few range balls. Now it's about 7:10 and still no sign of Canseco. We start to walk toward the course and just then, we hear tires screeching in the parking lot. This big guy (Canseco is about six-four, 240) gets out of the car and I'm doing a double take. You could hear that whoever it was already had on cleats. He grabs a bag and when he gets within 50 yards, I can see it's Canseco. If you can picture it, he's dressed in Spandex shorts, like bicycle riders wear. He's wearing a sweatshirt cut off in two places, so you can see his biceps and his navel and he's got on long, white sanitary socks, like we wear on the diamond, pulled up over his knees. He's got on Oakley sunglasses and a hat flipped up, and along with all that, he's got on two wristbands and two batting gloves. His spikes are more like wrestling boots that come halfway up his shins. And here he comes, up to the first tee at The Country Club. I drop all my clubs there on the course and make a beeline for him before he can get out here. I told him he'd have to drop about four hundred dollars in the pro shop before he can even get onto the driving range. Ever since then, he's the best-dressed golfer around. He's really got the fever and loves golf.

I enjoy watching other pitchers and how they handle adversity, and that's probably the thing I enjoy most about watching and playing with different golfers in pro-ams. Some guys get a little fire in their eyes and you can really see it. With other guys, it looks like they're just trying to hang on. I can relate that to baseball. You see guys out there who probably have a great deal of talent, but they never apply it. Just standing in the same fairway as some of the greatest golfers on tour definitely helped me. It taught me how to really manage myself on a golf course instead of constantly grinding and trying to hit it hard and make birdies. That's how I was able to improve. Athletic ability and eye-hand coordination may be somewhat responsible, but there's nothing like learning from the best.

I've learned the same way about pitching and being in the big leagues. I was fortunate enough to play with Tom Seaver when he was with Boston in 1986. You listen and learn and you can absorb a lot. Of course, playing with PGA Tour pros can be intimidating, too. You put your ball on the ground and look over and see three or four golfers who are among the best in the world. You're in their office. So all of a sudden, you are trying to put a real pretty swing on the ball, because they are all standing there, eyeing you, from your grip to finish.

Obviously, I love to pitch and play the game of baseball, but for being out of your own element, golf is probably the best game I know. The link between golf and baseball is really all about concentration. Playing in tournaments after January, when you're coming up on spring training, you really have to concentrate. If you don't focus, you are going to embarrass yourself out there. That's true in baseball and in golf.

ALICE COOPER

Alice Cooper is the original King of Shock Rock. As the ringmaster of the ultimate heavy-metal horror circus, Cooper's live shows featured huge snakes, guillotines, explosions, and lots of fake blood. The over-the-top performances made him one of the most popular recording artists of the 1970s, as songs like "School's Out" and "No More Mr. Nice Guy" reached the top of the charts. Cooper continues to record and perform, maintaining his substantial cult following. He also plays golf. That is not a typo. Alice Cooper is a two handicap.

Actually, I started playing golf as an alternative to alcoholism. I mean, I had hacked around a little bit before, but when I stopped drinking twenty years ago, I learned quickly that an alcoholic's worst enemy is time. When an alcoholic gets up in the morning, you make a drink and that starts your day. So the deal was, now that I'm straight, I have to find something that's going to take time. I decided golf would be a good four hours, and I always did like to play. It was one of those things where it was thirty-six holes a day for a year. I'd get up in the morning, my wife would point to my clubs and say: "Go. I don't want to see you till six o'clock tonight." I ended up being a nine handicap by the end of that year. And it's just carried over since then. I play six times a week, almost every single morning.

People have to understand that I'm probably one of the most successful schizophrenics in the world. At night, I completely change my image, and I become Alice Cooper, this insane monster on stage that the audience would never picture having a golf club in his hand. I become a character who, if you put a golf club in his hand, would see it as some kind of martial arts weapon. But as soon as I'm done performing, that's it. The same guy wakes up in the morning and thinks: "Where am I playing golf today?"

It's funny—thirty years ago, I would have laughed if you told me that all the rock rebels of the time would eventually turn into single-digit or scratch golfers, including me. After all we went through, you'd think we'd be too burned out to play—it really is amazing. Look at the guys who are still around—Neil Young, Bob Dylan, Iggy Pop, Lou Reed—they all love golf. It's so weird to see Lou Reed and Iggy Pop on a golf course—even I sense how bizarre that is. The two most underground characters in America, and Lou's coming over to me saying, "Hey, Alice, I'm pushing the ball right. What am I doing wrong?"

And I say, "You just got to let your hands finish."

Very strange. The last time I had seen Lou was in Max's Kansas City with all the Andy Warhol gang and all kinds of crazy stuff going on in the background, and now we're talking about . . . golf.

I've got two days that I'd say are tied for my best day in golf. One was at Pine Valley. I'd never been there before, but I had an off day during a concert tour, and Ely Callaway got me on the course. I didn't know who I was going play with. I ended up playing with a couple of members who I didn't know. The caddie master, who's an old Scottish guy, carried my bag. The first thing he said to me was, "Listen, sonny"—and I immediately liked the guy—"what's your handicap?" And I said: "Seven." And he says, "Okay, well, the standing rule around here is that you don't break 85 your first time out."

I said, "Okay, I'm just happy to be here." So we went around, and he had a poem about every single hole that he would recite on the tee, which I thought was great. I shot 73! Never missed a fairway, never missed a green. And the caddie master goes into the men's grill and says: "I just can't believe this. This skinny little rock 'n' roll guy comes out and shoots 73. We've got to do something! We've got to make the course harder!"

It was just one of those days that everything I hit was just solid right down the middle. I was pulling every club at the right time. Now, what the caddie master doesn't know is that the next day, I played a dinky public course in Ohio and shot 81. That just tells you a lot about the game of golf.

The other great day, I played with three pros at my home course, which is Camelback Golf Club in Scottsdale, Arizona. I got to the last hole—we were playing skins—and on the tee of the par-5 I said: "What do I need here? I know I'm playing pretty good." One of my playing partners says: "You par this hole, you make 69."

I was shocked. I'd never broken 70 before. But I looked at the card and it was true. So I hit my drive, hit my second shot over the green, and chipped in for eagle. Total score of 67, and seventeen skins, and I walked away and gave the guys all their money back. I said, "Just sign my card. I am now Mr. 67."

When I got down to a two handicap not that long ago, I asked a couple of senior pros what the next level is like, just out of curiosity. Bruce Fleisher told me: "If you actually were ever serious about this, you would need to take a year off, maybe two, and go with David Leadbetter or someone of his caliber and just give your whole game to him. A lot of guys have got raw talent, but let's see if you can shape it into a guy that can shoot 68 every day. Don't just try to go out there and go after your card, because you'll embarrass yourself. You'll be playing under tremendous pressure with these guys."

See, what he's forgetting is if I went out on the Senior Tour, I would try to finish in the middle of the pack, but I'd make ten million dollars a year in endorsements, because of the novelty of Alice Cooper in competitive golf! Believe me, I would push the envelope of what's appropriate golf wear, and I think it would sell a lot of tickets. I think, though, if you can play the game well enough, show business is your best friend. Dennis Rodman can have purple hair because he gets fifteen, twenty rebounds a night. If you can back up some ridiculous thing that you do, then do it. I would love to get out there and try it, because the pros know I'm not a threat. I would love to finish in the top ten once or twice in my life. Those guys are the most special players in the world. I'd be comic relief. Nobody would know where I'd hid the snake. And I wouldn't take money out of anybody's pocket. They'd probably say, "Hey, I don't care if he wears makeup, if he can shoot 69, let him play." I would never do anything to disgrace the game, but I feel if you can play the game at a high level, why not make it more fun? Why not make it less stodgy?

With that in mind, I thought I'd mention a great game some friends and I invented called Psychoskins. In Psychoskins, you have to have a par or better to win. Let's say you birdie a hole and you get six skins. You have to have the lowest score on the next hole or at least tie with the lowest score in order to collect. In other words, you have to at least par the next hole. But let's say you're putting for par, and you have six skins riding. The rule is that the other guys are allowed to do anything to distract you, other than get in your line or physically touch you. So, there are times when a guy's got 12 skins on the line, he's got a five-foot putt, and there are guys with their pants down around their ankles, mooning him, screaming at him, shaking the flag, anything to distract him. They go psycho, and that's the name of the game. Eight out of ten times, he'll miss that five-foot putt, and that's what makes it great. Depending on what course you're on, it's usually better to play when there aren't that many other groups around. If you have the right situation, though, it turns serious competition into a laugh riot.

One of the funniest things I ever saw in my life was on the golf course. Scott Flansberg is a guy I play with every day—he does those late-night infomercials for Mathmagic. So we were playing our home course, and he's wearing this loose shirt and loose shorts, and this huge black bumblebee comes at him and drops down into his shirt. He's allergic to stings, so he panics. I have never seen anybody react so wildly. His clubs go flying up in the air, he pulls his shirt off and is dancing around—it was pretty serious, so we shouldn't have been laughing, but we were anyway. Then we hear the buzzing again, and he thinks the bee has traveled into his pants! So now he's jumping and flailing around with his pants down, and it's still going *bzzz, bzzz.*

Turns out his cell phone was in the pocket of his shorts, and he had set it to buzz. Not the bee. And I said: "Hey, I think your phone's ringing." Can you imagine? Do you think we ever let him live this down? No, of course not, not to this very day.

TOM DeLAY

Tom DeLay has represented the twenty-second district in the state of Texas since 1984, and is currently the House Majority Leader in the 108th Congress. One of the most significant functions of this position is in setting the agenda—selecting which bills the House will consider and the timing of their consideration. DeLay is considered one of the most skillful hands in promoting the Republican agenda in Congress, lending his voice to domestic and foreign policy issues in equal measure. When Congress is not in session, DeLay enjoys spending time with his family—he and his wife recently became grandparents—and working on his golf game on the side.

I was raised for part of my childhood in Venezuela, and the Americans lived in what were called Oil Company Camps. They weren't typical camps with tents; they were pretty nice homes, and each company camp had a country club. Part of the country club's program, of course, was that they gave golf lessons to the kids. So I started taking lessons when I was eight years old, and a couple of years later I started caddying for the adults. When they finished playing the caddies would go out on the course and play. So that's really how I got started with the game.

Today, I tell people my handicap is politics—before I got into politics, my handicap was around six, now it's closer to ten. I have no native talent—everything has to come from hard work.

Luckily, the lessons I took as a kid were very good, so that gave me fundamentals that I've always stuck to, and allowed me to usually correct my own problems along the way, though I have taken a few lessons when something came up that I couldn't fix.

My best day in golf was undoubtedly winning the club championship at the little local club that I belonged to before I got involved in politics. I was just out of college and trying to build my own business, so I couldn't afford a really upscale country club, so I joined a place called Valley Lodge Club in Simonton, Texas. It was just a little nine-hole course, but we had a great golf program there. One day I decided I was going to be the club champion, so I spent a solid year, seven days a week, hitting balls, playing, practicing almost every day. Instead of going to lunch, I'd break at noon, go hit balls, then after work I'd return to the course and either hit balls or play practically every evening. Then on the weekends, I'd play in all the various tournaments we had going, all leading up to the club championship weekend.

Finally the big weekend came and I played what I thought was pretty disappointing golf. The first day, I believe I shot an 80, and the next day an 81, so I really thought I was out of it. But the guy who was my primary challenger just blew up on the second day after an opening round 75, and we wound up tied. We played a four-hole sudden-death match on the third day, and I played probably the greatest golf I've every played in my life. The fourth hole was a short par-4 with a big ditch in front of the green where most the time people would usually lay up with a three-wood, and I managed to drive the green with that club. The adrenaline was flowing, and on that day it worked to my advantage. My opponent hit his drive off into the brush and found his second shot offered no chance of recovery. He conceded the hole and the club championship. That was easily my best day in golf. Of course, everybody forgot about it the next day, but I didn't. I've still got the trophy at home. It's actually a pretty ugly piece of hardware, but I'm extremely proud of it.

I'd have to say close second was the thrill of playing with my idol, Arnold Palmer, last year at Bay Hill. Unfortunately, it turned out to be horrible day—cold, blustery, and drizzly, not at all Florida weather. It shows you what a great guy he is, though—he played, and he absolutely hates playing in nasty weather. He could have very easily just blown it off, but we walked sixteen holes together as foursome with his son-in-law and Tom Feeney, former Speaker of the House in Florida. I think Arnold knows exactly how much it means for people to just have that one round in his company—and it's not an ego thing, it's simply his way of giving back to the game. He's a man of extremely deep moral character, and that shows in his golf and in the way he's handled his success. I have nothing but admiration for him, and I'll be telling people about that round for the rest of my life, I'm sure.

When I have the time to spare, I also really enjoy playing with some of my colleagues in Washington. I think the most fun I've had in recent memory was teaming up with President Bush last year in a match at Andrews Air Force Base against two other congressmen, Dan Burton of Indiana and Mike Oxley of Ohio. We beat them, and everyone played pretty well, despite the media attention that we drew. And in the Bush tradition, we naturally played very quickly. It was one of the fastest matches I've had.

That was a fairly informal match—at least as far as playing with a head of state can be—but we also play an annual tournament organized with the Republicans and Democrats. It's just straightforward tournament match play. There's also a trophy for low gross, which I won a few years ago. It's a lot of fun—the competition is strong, and there are strong golfers on both sides of the aisle. We have some very good golfers on our side. Right now the Republicans have a sophomore from New Jersey named Mike Ferguson who's pretty close to scratch— he's probably the best golfer in the House. It's a great year for the Republicans. We control Congress, the White House, and bragging rights as the best golfers.

Golf definitely goes a long way toward understanding what kind of character you have. A game that's played on the honor system means that you can often recognize someone with less than stellar integrity. I happen to be a very aggressive golfer—

a Palmer trait that I've emulated—and I'm a rules man. It sort of dovetails with my role in the House; I'm a strict constitutionalist—there are rules and you have to play by them. All members, on the golf course and in Congress, have to work under the same parameters, otherwise the game becomes confused and basically meaningless.

CELINE DION

Pop star Celine Dion caught the golf bug from her husband, who has played the game for three decades. Although a newcomer to the game, she already owns one golf course, Le Mirage, near her native Montreal, Canada. Celine is excited to sample the best golf in Las Vegas when she has a break from her smash-hit show "A New Day" at Caesars Palace.

About five years ago, after René insisted for the tenth time that I should consider playing golf—that it would be a passion that we could share together—I decided to give it a try. I told him I wasn't going out there until he got me some lessons, so he gave me a month of vacation and I took some lessons, and of course, I got hooked. But I still need time to take more lessons and play a lot more.

The thing that's surprised me about playing golf is how similar it is to performing. When I get ready to sing a song, I have to concentrate, I have to focus, and I have to compete with myself. I'm not competing with others. And I have to be the best. When I'm on the golf course and I get ready to hit the ball, I concentrate and then I focus and then on my backswing, I'm just getting ready to do my best, like hitting my best note.

It's just an incredible feeling seeing the ball go forever after you hit it and you are really in competition with yourself, even when you are playing with others. It's wonderful to be in contact with nature also. I'm not into sports a lot, but golf has been really relaxing for me.

As far as my best day in golf, there have been a few best days already, even though I've been a golfer for just around five years. My first best day was probably during one of my first lessons. I hit the ball and I experienced that great feeling you get when you swing right, make solid contact, and the ball goes up in the air, the way it's supposed to. That was a great feeling. The other day I like to think about was not too long ago when I beat my husband at golf for the first time. And even though I've only been playing a little while, I've been fortunate enough to play with some really great golfers like Annika Sorenstam, Jesper Parnevik, and Greg Norman. I haven't played with Jack Nicklaus, Phil Mickelson, or Tiger Woods, but we were lucky enough to meet them and have lovely dinners with them and their families.

I don't know if it's that unusual, but I've hit a bird and I thought I had a birdie. But that's not quite it, is it? It was at the Desert Inn in Las Vegas. I hit my second shot with a five-iron and missed most of the ball. It hit a pretty good-sized bird, not as big as a Canadian goose, but pretty big. The bird was okay, his legs were a little shaky, so I stayed with it a few minutes and then we had to go, because the people behind us wanted to play. I was shaking for about a half hour after hitting that poor bird, but people tell me that happens a lot on the golf course.

Some people say that playing golf changes people. I don't know if that's true, but I do know that every time you play golf, you learn a little more about yourself. You can get really mad playing golf, and when you lose your temper, it can be kind of telling. Golf teaches you a lesson about behaving, about being good and not just losing it out there when things go badly. I mean, you learn, or you should learn, to hold your temper, because there will be always be another shot. You just can't let the game destroy you, because it can drive you crazy. So you have to behave yourself. Golf teaches you to relax and, maybe not change your personality completely, but it definitely teaches you more control and self-discipline. Those are important in whatever you are doing. Maybe that's why so many people love golf, even while it's driving them crazy.

PETE DYE

Pete Dye is one of the top golf-course designers working today. Over the course of his career, Dye's expressive designs have won numerous awards. A number of them, like Harbour Town, the Stadium Course at La Quinta, Kingsmill, and the TPC at Sawgrass are famous stops on the PGA Tour. With an assist from his wife, Alice, Pete has influenced the future of golf course design known today as Target Golf. Pete plays only ten or twelve times a year, but manages to keep his handicap hovering somewhere between four and eight.

Early in the 1960s I was a USGA committee member for the Greens Section, and I met a gentleman who wanted to build a nine-hole golf course. I did not know anything about golf architecture, but my bride, Alice, and I had always been interested in golf, so we took him up on the offer, and we built a nine-hole course named Eldorado in Indiana. The following year, the president of the University of Michigan, Dr. Harlan Hatcher, was driving through Indiana and stopped to play the nine-hole course. Later, he telephoned me and said, "We're going to be starting a major project in Ann Arbor for the University of Michigan. I would be interested in talking to you about designing and building the golf course." I told him I was in the insurance business, I did not have any real experience, and I did not know how to draw up plans, and so on. He said: "Come up and talk to me anyway." To make a long story short,

I built Raderick Farm for the University of Michigan, and I've been doing it ever since—two a year over a period of forty years. Most of my competitors design twenty courses a year.

Choosing the favorite course I have designed is the question I'm asked most often. There is no right answer. It's kind of like choosing between the kids; they're all different. I have always kind of liked the work I did down in the Dominican Republic because I started the project. I was shown the ocean-front land that was 35 miles from even a paved road, and now there are four golf courses, and Teeth of the Dog is rated one of the greatest in the world. There are fifty thousand people working for the resort and the area developed around those courses. I've always felt that the course I built for the PGA Tour, the TPC at Sawgrass, has held together pretty good over the years. That course received a lot of notoriety for the island green on the 17th hole. I've always liked that course and Harbour Town, but every course offers something different.

Every round offers something different too. One day, many years ago, I was having lunch with three guests at Seminole Golf Club, and George Coleman, who was the club president at the time, came over and asked me if I would like to play with Ben Hogan. With my guests sitting right there, I looked up at him, and said, "Yes, sir, I'd be glad to." Fortunately, I was able to pawn my guests off on another member so that they could play that day.

At that time Henry Picard was the golf professional at Seminole. I went down to the little shop and on display there was a set of Hogan Medallion irons. I took them and went around the corner to the caddie pen, and I beat them against the cement floor, kicked them, did everything I could to scar them up as best as I could, so they'd look well used. I hit a few practice shots and set out on the course with Mr. Hogan and George Coleman. When we started, my hands were wet; I was so nervous, I do not remember hitting my drive. But after that round I got to know Mr. Hogan, and played with him several times over the next few years. These were my best golf days because he always was my idol. The second year, when I went back, he looked in my bag and said: "I see you've still have those Medallions." So playing with Mr. Hogan at Seminole were my best days in golf.

I remember he was still playing incredible golf during those years in the late 1960s. One time I'll never forget was playing a round with him, George Coleman, and the great amateur Billy Joe Patton. On the dogleg right 16th hole of Seminole, the wind was coming dead out of the east, and Hogan hit a pretty good drive into the teeth of the wind, then a terrific two-iron onto the green. George Coleman says to him, "Ben, that was a great shot."

And by that time I had played with him long enough that I was finally able to get my nerve up to say something. So I said: "No, that was just a routine two-iron." Hogan kind of looked up at me, and I think he got a kick out of it, because when he won the Open with that famous two-iron shot, someone complimented him and Hogan replied, "That was just a routine two-iron."

Billy Joe Patton had seen the shot from several yards away and he said, "Ben, I know damn well you're going to want to tell somebody about that shot tonight." I said: "Valerie won't want to hear about it, so I'm going to give you my number, and you can call me." And Hogan broke up laughing. Without a doubt, those were my favorite days.

People always ask me about the island green at Sawgrass, so I'll set the record straight here—it was my bride, Alice's, idea. When we were building the course, we found the site didn't have much sand, but it had tons of clay. In Florida, you think everything's sand, but that's not the case. So we were constantly digging deep holes looking for sand, and finally we found a big pocket of the sand and dug it all out. Then we realized all of a sudden that there was no room to form a green. That was when Alice said, "Why don't you pile all the mud back in there and make an island green?" I listened to her, and it was probably the smartest thing I have ever done in my life.

The last thing I want to mention here is something that I've been talking about for quite some time now, and I believe it's important to the future of the sport. Golf needs a uniform ball. One day the general public is going to figure out that the manufacturers are not doing anything for them, and there is going to be a rebellion. The reason is that these premium golf balls only help pros with extremely high swing speeds. John Daly can't possibly be any stronger than he was ten years ago, but he is averaging 24 yards further, and the difference is the ball. But for ladies who hit the ball 134 to 140 yards, there is not a ball on the market, in my opinion, that goes one inch further for them than the ones made fifty years ago. The same goes for the average senior man. The clubs and shafts are greatly improved, but not the ball, unless you swing over a hundred miles an hour. Well, why are they helping the professionals? All it does is turn our greatest courses into pitch-'n'-putts. All the other major sports use a uniform ball—golf should too.

The way this happened is very simple. The manufacturers make a lot of money, obviously, and they go out and find aerospace engineers working eighty hours a week trying to shoot a man to Mars and back, and they tell him: "Come work for us, we'll double your pay. All you need to do is get this little ball to travel a few more yards and conform to the USGA standards." The aerospace engineer finds a way within a short time—the physics just aren't very challenging for him compared to what he was doing before.

The problem is that the USGA does not have the money to fight the manufacturers. Unless Congress gets involved and passes a law, the countersuits will absolutely kill the USGA. Deane Beman tried like the devil to outlaw the square grooves made by Karsten Solheim of Ping. He did not have the backing of the USGA or the PGA and was never able to get control of the ball or golf club. In the end, the result is that a major part of the game has been glossed over. Professionals almost never have to hit long irons anymore. On a par 4, you will not see those long-iron clubs used unless there is a windstorm. In the past, the truly great players—Hogan, Nicklaus, and all—were highly skilled long-iron players. From a spectator's point of view, you want to see a pro hit a driver and then a normal shot toward the green, but when a 470-yard hole plays more like 420, you're most likely to see a long iron on his tee shot than anything else.

You saw proof of this during the 2002 Ryder Cup more than anywhere else. Americans don't fully develop their talents because they are not pushed to hit four-irons into long par 4s, or putt on slower greens. They go over to Europe and find the greens are slower and grainier, and they cannot putt to save their lives. I understand the game has changed. I remember reading old books from forty years ago, complaining about the ball carrying too far. But today, when I see the PGA Tour slogan, "These Guys Are Good," it's hard for me not to think it's more like, "These Guys Got It Easy."

KEN EICHELE

New York City firefighter Ken Eichele is, by his own description, "the most overexposed average guy you'll ever meet. . . . Andy Warhol was wrong in my case, my fifteen minutes of fame have been more like three hours." Eichele, a competitive amateur golfer, happened to be qualifying for the U.S. Mid-Amateur on September 11, 2001. Propelled into the spotlight by the events of that day, Eichele has proven to be a thoughtful and engaging spokesman for the FDNY. We are proud to have him as a contributor to this book, and would like to take a moment to thank the members of the FDNY, NYPD, and PAPD for their courage and hard work on that tragic day, and beyond.

I grew up in Queens, across the street from Kissena Golf Course, one of the city's public courses. There was nothing between the course and my house at the time, just a bridle path, some vacant lots, and swampland with turtles and rabbits and all kinds of creatures running around. When I was about six years old, I noticed some of the older kids used to go and hop the fence at night. My father let me go on to the course with some of the ones that he trusted. The Parks Department employees went home around four P.M., and after that we'd just go play. I continued doing it right through college. Friends came and went, some guys played and lost interest, but I was always there. Eventually, I was playing alone a lot of nights.

My mother always used to say: "I never worried about him. I always knew where he was."

I started playing more competitively as a teenager, in skins games where I was basically the only white guy out there. The pro at Kissena at the time was a black man, and a lot of good black players were regulars at the course. I'd go down the fairway with anywhere between seven and eleven guys, all of them older than me. If you were out of the hole, you picked up. That really honed my competitiveness, and got me to learn how to play aggressively and stay in the hole. When you play skins games, nothing matters except birdies. I was a kid without a lot of money, and it was possible to win the kind of money that was pretty significant to me at the time. You never lost a lot, but you could win a lot—that's the way skins is. The only regret that I have from that time is that I wish I'd had some formal training. I developed some bad habits, particularly with my grip, that took me years and years to fix.

When I became a member of the fire department, I quickly realized that it's the ideal career for playing competitive golf on the side, because a firefighter's schedule is very flexible. You can usually switch shifts with someone if you have a tournament on Tuesday, say. You usually work twenty-four hours on, seventy-two off, so you have a lot of time during the week to play. If you know the New York metropolitan area, golf during the week is a lot easier to manage than on the weekends. So it worked out really well for me as far continuing to improve my game.

I try to play 150 rounds a year at maybe fifty different courses. In the last five years, I've started playing through the winter, so that adds to the number. Before they came out with Gore-Tex and Polarfleece, I had to wear a winter coat out there, and it made swinging a club difficult. But now I love winter golf. A couple of years ago I drove out onto Long Island just looking for a course that was open, and when I finally found one, the guys working there just looked at me like I was crazy. I had a great time, though. The course was empty and I'd play three or four balls on every hole, just practicing different shots.

As far as golf experiences go, there are really three of them that stand out in my mind. One is the first time I ever played

Fisher's Island. My friend invited me there, and that is such a great golf experience, and a beautiful place. You take a boat across Long Island Sound to get there, and when you arrive you feel like you've just stepped into this mystical kind of place. I had played Pebble Beach before that, and Fisher's Island makes Pebble Beach look ugly, in my opinion. It's so quiet, and every hole on the course would be a signature hole somewhere else.

From a competitive standpoint, I'll always remember the North-South Senior at Pinehurst, and it would be the best memory by far if it had turned out a little differently. It's a national tournament, a lot of big-name amateurs play in it, and I came in second. For a while, it looked like I was going to win. On the last day of the event, the leaders play together, obviously, and they put us out there with a shotgun start, which is unusual. The organizers' reasoning made sense, though—they wanted everybody to go to the awards ceremony. A lot of times, guys will just leave if they haven't played well, and there's no one left to congratulate the winner. So they decided everyone should finish at the same time.

After nine holes, an official came up to my group and said: "It's only you four left. Everybody else is out of the running." After fourteen holes, I was three behind the leader, and he hit a shot ten feet from the pin on the 15th hole, which is a long par-3. I hit the pin and made a three-foot putt, while the other guy missed his. Then I birdied 15, 16, and 17, and by that time I'm one up going to the last hole. I had about a seven-foot putt, and I was getting nervous. But any competitive player will tell you: You're never not going to be nervous, so you have to learn to produce good shots regardless. Anyway, my playing partner missed his birdie putt, so at that point I thought I just needed a two-putt to win. So I lagged it up nice and easy, about two inches short, sunk the putt, and everybody started shaking my hand, photographers were taking my picture, and so on. And about ten minutes later, this guy comes in and puts his card on the table. He had shot four or five under in the back nine, holing out two shots from the fairway for eagles, and beat me by a shot. I wish the guy I was playing with had sunk his putt, in retrospect, because then I wouldn't have played it safe, thinking that a two-putt would win it. Finishing second in a national tournament is something I'm really proud of, but knowing that for ten minutes I was the winner takes a little of the luster off that second-place finish.

On September 11, 2001, I was qualifying for the U.S. Mid-Amateur in Bedford, New York. I had an early morning start, and I was even par after nine holes. On the ninth green, a friend of mine, Dave Segot, who's also a city firefighter, came over to me and said, "A plane hit the Trade Center."

I was stunned. I said, "What do you mean? What kind of plane?" Dave said he didn't know, but the people who were arriving for the afternoon rounds were saying it was just a Piper Cub. So I was concerned, but didn't think it was something I had to run back to the city for. On the 14th hole, another guy I play with over at Clearview, Pat Reilly, says to me: "The Twin Towers are gone."

I didn't believe him at first, but I could tell he was serious. I said, "Forget it. I've gotta get down there."

"You can't. They closed the bridges. You can't get back."

After that point, the rest of the day was a blur. They canceled the tournament and told everyone to come in off the course. We gathered around a TV in the locker room just as they were starting to show the footage of the Towers collapsing. Dave and I looked at each other and said, "God, we just lost hundreds of guys." We knew right away. If the buildings had collapsed immediately, there would have been tens of thousands of fatalities, but not as many firemen. I said, "We've gotta get back. I don't care if the bridges are closed, we'll bull our way across."

We managed to get into Queens via the Throgs Neck Bridge, so I was able to stop at home for a moment to call a family member. I asked him to call the rest of my family to tell them I was okay. Then I grabbed a few changes of clothes, because I knew I wouldn't be going home for a while. After trying several of the Bronx bridges and getting turned away, I finally got over the Willis Avenue Bridge. There were people on foot, hundreds of them walking shoulder to shoulder, but I drove slowly and they parted for me.

When I finally got in to work, the other chiefs told me they needed me to stay behind in case anything happened uptown—there was no one from the department left up there. So I didn't get downtown until later that night. I stayed there for almost the next twenty-four hours, searching for people. That entire night we didn't find anyone alive, but the next afternoon around one o'clock we found a woman who had been trapped, and she was the last person found alive. She wasn't that badly injured, either. Janelle was her name, and all she could say when we found her was: "I want some water, I want some water." It's just amazing that a few people survived. In the end, we lost nine guys from my house alone. Looking back on that event, it's not surprising that the terrorists would try it again after the bombing in '93. A lot of people in New York had the sense it was still a target, and it's just unfortunate and tragic that they were right.

It's funny—my sisters always used to say, "You play too much golf." But now they say, "I'll never, ever give you a hard time about playing golf again, because it's what saved you." And they're right. I said pretty much the same thing when the Golf Channel filmed me and three of my friends—two firemen and a cop—about a month after 9/11 for a show called *New York Stories*. One of the things I said was that golf really is a great escape. A lot of the people who were involved in the recovery, obviously, were really traumatized by feelings of depression and a kind of guilt that they had lived when so many of their friends did not. I've experienced some of those things myself, but while golf isn't a cure-all by any stretch of the imagination, I'm glad that the game is a part of my life. The friendships that I've made through the game mean an awful lot to me, and to be able to get out on the course and enjoy the company of the guys in the fire and police departments is something I wouldn't trade for anything.

LEE ELDER

Lee Elder won four PGA Tour events and eight Senior PGA Tour events over the course of a long career. He was the first African American man ever to reach the million-dollar earnings mark, after Arnold Palmer, but his impact on the game of golf can also be measured as a pioneer. Elder was the first African American ever to play in the Masters, the Ryder Cup, and the first integrated tournament in apartheid South Africa, in 1971. In an era when the greatest golfer in the world is multiracial, it's important to remember that the doors Tiger Woods has smashed through were first opened by men like Lee Elder, Charlie Sifford, and Ted Rhodes. Today, Elder continues to play golf as well as work with his charitable foundation. He is also at work on his autobiography.

My interest in golf arrived through caddying, which I started when I was twelve years old. I was born in Dallas, Texas, and I caddied at Tennison Park, which was not too far from my home. In those days, though, my opportunities to practice were limited to Mondays, because it wasn't until 1956 that golf courses became integrated. On Mondays the public courses opened up, but as a young kid, I had to go with someone. I learned a lot from watching other people play.

Then, of course, as I got older I became aware of Ted Rhodes and Charlie Sifford, who were both playing well on the Tour, even though there were still many tournaments that didn't let them play. I looked up to them a lot, and realized if they could do it then I could too. My confidence grew, and I started taking a lot of small steps along the way.

There's no doubt in my mind, the 1979 Ryder Cup stands out as the most significant moment in my career. Almost from the day that I qualified to play on the Tour, so many guys had talked with me about it, saying how much of an honor it is to be able to represent your country. By playing well over a two-year period, I accumulated enough points through the PGA Championship at Oakland Hills that I qualified for the Ryder Cup team. That Sunday, upon learning I'd made the team, was one of the most joyful times I've ever had. It far outweighed anything else that I had done—even qualifying to play at Augusta did not measure up to representing my country. Almost immediately, congratulatory letters began to arrive, and that certainly made me very happy because it was something that I had wanted for such a long period of time.

The Ryder Cup that year was played at the Greenbrier in West Virginia. On the first morning I was paired up in four-ball competition with Andy Bean, playing against Nick Faldo and Peter Oosterhuis. When we saw the slate, all my teammates said, "Oh man, you guys have drawn the toughest match." Faldo was a truly great player, obviously, but Oosterhuis! Although he struggled somewhat on the PGA Tour, he had been a lights-out golfer in the Ryder Cup throughout the entire decade. It struck me that this match was pretty much two unknowns facing two giants, guys with a lot of experience.

We won that opening match 2 and 1, which was a big lift for the U.S. team. The U.S. won three of the four morning matches, which really set the tone for the entire event. The Europeans spent the rest of the time trying to catch us.

I would have had a much harder time being a rookie in the Ryder Cup if it wasn't for the fact that I had perhaps the greatest captain that you could ask for in Billy Casper. He was able to tell you so much about the Ryder Cup and the way he wanted you to play that I went out with a very clear sense of what I needed to do from shot to shot. Casper always tried to keep us calm after every match with short team meetings. Usually his message was to relax, not put too much pressure on yourself. Casper would ask how you felt about a match—your opponent's tendencies, certain places on the course that might concern you—and his advice was always solid, and above all, encouraging.

The third day in singles play I was matched against Nick Faldo. Even though I lost the match, it's one of my most memorable rounds for the sheer intensity of the competition. In fact, I was 2 up on him on the front nine, and I felt very strongly that I was going to win the match. I was playing well, and had him in the position where I wanted him to be. On the par-3 9th hole, I almost made a hole in one with a two-iron from about 200 yards, and the birdie put me 2 up. I remember the roar of the crowd—it was loud enough to attract a huge gallery watching us when we made the turn. But Faldo played a phenomenal back nine. I shot one under par on the back nine, and I think he shot about five under. He just had a lot of fine, clean shots to produce a victory. It was a very good, close match. At the end of the day, we won the Ryder Cup 17–11, though a lot of the matches were a lot closer than the final score indicates. Standing with my American teammates with the trophy, knowing that I had represented my country well, was far and away my best day in golf.

TOM FAZIO

Tom Fazio is one of the premier golf course designers working today. In the 2002 version of Golf Digest's *prestigious annual poll of the 100 Greatest Courses in America, ten of Fazio's designs made the list, led by Steve Wynn's Shadow Creek, a desert course outside Las Vegas that, like the city itself, was created from nothing. Over the past four decades he has been involved in the creation of around two hundred golf courses, making him also one of the most prolific designers ever. Today, the seven-handicap Fazio continues to churn out one innovative design after another, and recently summarized his career and design philosophy in a book entitled* Golf Course Designs.

I grew up in a golfing family. My father was a club professional and my uncle, George Fazio, was a touring professional. He won a few tournaments, but wasn't a major-name player. He lost the 1950 U.S. Open in a playoff to Ben Hogan at Merion, after Hogan had come back from a bus accident. I often wonder if things would have turned out differently had Uncle George won that event, because after he stopped playing on the PGA Tour, he got involved in the golf operations business and got his family involved, then started creating his own golf courses in the late fifties, which was when I started working with him.

My best day in golf may have been one that didn't happen. I did a course called Caves Valley near Baltimore in the early nineties, and I was invited to play there with George H. W. Bush, who was president at the time; Reg Murphy, who was president of the USGA; and Arnold Palmer. It wasn't an official opening or anything, just a casual game—with two presidents and a king. I agreed to come, but when they told me the date was going to be a Saturday, I couldn't go. I have a rule with my wife that I don't do weekends anywhere for any amount of money or for any reason. I have six children, so the rule makes a lot of sense when it comes to them. My youngest daughter was playing in a soccer match that day, so I called back and told them I couldn't make it. My daughter found out about it later and told all her friends how crazy I was to skip golf with the president just to see her soccer game. Business is important, sure, but if you keep putting it before your family, it becomes a habit. And my daughter scored the only two goals in the game, so I would have been so mad at myself if I hadn't been there.

My best day in golf that actually *did* happen was taking my three sons—Logan, Gavin, and Austin—to Pelican Hill, an ocean-front course in Newport Beach, California. Nothing comes close to its beauty. We played thirty-six that day, and it occurred to me that it was the first time I'd ever taken all three of them at the same time and actually made a golf date somewhere other than at home. The thing that I remember the most about it was the camaraderie. All day, I kept saying to myself, *Thank you, God, for making this happen.* I remember the days when we were building that course, and it never dawned on me that someday I'd be able to bring my sons there. Taking them to a golf course that I designed, one of them put an arm around me and said: "Dad, how many courses have you designed? We've got to play them all." So I set that as a goal, and we've been working on it for a few years now.

I think it's a different world than it used to be, as far as golf and families go. My dad was a golfer, and I would caddie for him when I was a youngster, but it was a different kind of thing. It wasn't seen as an opportunity to forge really great relationships with your kids, but when you're involved with the game with your family, rather than using is as an escape from your family, the enjoyment you can have reaches a whole new level. I take my oldest son to Pine Valley every July to play in the father-son, and that's the highlight of my golf year. The only asterisk I put on it is that my other two sons are not there.

I'm often asked what my process is in moving a design from concept to finished product. The short answer is that there is no set process, but the thing that always goes through my mind is what a hole in its setting would be like for all levels of players. I'm interested in how golf is played by Tiger Woods, the greatest player in the world. I love to watch that kind of golf. But I also need to be aware of every other person after him, down to the beginners. That's the essence of my job, creating a product that will be liked by people of all abilities. It's easy to design a golf course to test Tiger Woods. But every time I plan a golf course, I'm always looking sideways. The length doesn't really matter to me; I'm more concerned about the width of a golf hole. The fact that I learned golf from my uncle, who was such a good player, I started out looking at it very differently, because those guys don't miss by much. But gradually I learned that the side-to-side approach was what makes the game great for everyone else. The object of the design game is also to create something of beauty, and the means to that end have changed significantly since I started in the sixties. On one hand, there's a lot more money out there to invest in great golf courses. When I started, the rule of thumb was that you'd have $10,000 per hole, and that was the shoestring budget. On the other, you now have environmental constraints that make the process much more complicated. This industry is like any other—we have laws that you have to abide by, it just happens that ours are on the environmental side. In many ways, I think they are actually a help to us, because golf courses today need much more acreage than they used to, because there are so many protected spaces that you're not allowed to touch. The result is a more open space—you don't see too many new courses with guys on the same fairway playing two different holes.

The other big question I'm often asked is how I was influenced by the architects of the past. It would sound good to say that I went and studied the old designers, but that wasn't the real world for me. I learned it from executing, from taking a piece of land and physically going out to build a golf course on the land you have to work with. It wasn't until the seventies or eighties that people even knew who Donald Ross or Alistair MacKenzie were. They weren't recognized until people started doing lists and rankings. On top of that, most of their courses bear very little resemblance to the ones they built all those years ago. The trees they planted have matured, and others have gone back and made changes to their bunkers and green complexes. A perfect example is Augusta National—the changes there, the lengthening of the course, has been the subject of so much debate lately. There are a lot of people who say it shouldn't be touched, but the truth is a course isn't fixed in time; it evolves very slowly and its relationship to the natural environment changes.

In this context, the changes are always based on improving the course to match how the game is played today. You can ask yourself the question that if MacKenzie and Jones had known that you could have a bent grass called A4 that could be cut as low and smooth as you want it, would they have made those greens as severe as they are today back in the thirties? Well, that's cocktail talk, because some people would say yes, others no.

What isn't up for debate is the fact that from tee to green, the technology available today produces incredible golf courses. I'm happy with the game as it is, but I would have said that in the Jack Nicklaus era, and I would have probably said that in the Bobby Jones era. Then we would have stopped at hickory shafts. The fundamentals of the game, however, don't change, and that's the most important thing.

I don't have a favorite among my own courses, but I do happen to be a Pine Valley fan. I think that Pine Valley is number one in the world. There are lots of factors behind it, but if I had to choose the setting for the perfect round of golf, it would be there. Mainly, it's a golfer's golf club. You go there for serious competition; you against the course, you against yourself or against your competitor. And it's just real golf in the sense that it's that competitive. It doesn't matter who you are—you can walk in the bar and see Arnold Palmer, who's a member, standing there, or it could be the new member from Seattle. It doesn't matter whether you're chairman of this or that, most people don't even know, much less care. They just care about teeing it up, and that's what is so wonderful about it.

And the golf course itself, the uniqueness of it, the fact that it is one of a kind and obviously a course that's been there through the test of time and people's memories. The Pine Valley experience just stands alone, going into that old building and seeing the same bar where people stood, put that foot on that rail and looked back at those same holes where they just made a great play or had their round fall to pieces—that's the nature of that golf course. It's not for everyone because it is penal, and extremely difficult, but for most people, it's precisely the kind of golf experience that lasts a lifetime.

TIM FINCHEM

Tim Finchem is the current commissioner of the PGA Tour. For almost a decade, he has worked on promoting golf around the world, as well as expanding earnings opportunities for PGA Tour members. Finchem has been instrumental in the formation of the International Federation of PGA Tours and the World Golf Foundation. He is a graduate of the University of Richmond and the University of Virginia Law School. Finchem lives in Florida with his wife and four children. He plays to a five handicap.

My dad was a sergeant in the Marine Corps down at Camp Lejeune, North Carolina, and he liked to play golf in his free time. I started following him around when I was about nine, hitting a shot here and there, just trying to get the ball airborne. When I was twelve and thirteen I played a lot at the base golf course. It was a buck to play all day, so that's how I got going. I was influenced by Arnold Palmer at the time. I tried to emulate his swing, and his play at the Masters really propelled my interest in the game. I also played a year of high-school golf, but after that year I knew it wasn't my ticket to college. I'm one of six kids, so I needed a scholarship. I shifted gears and went to college on a debate scholarship. Ever since then playing golf has been an avocation, although I have been fortunate enough, as fate would have it, to associate my career with the sport.

After college I practiced law for a while, spent some time in the government and in the consulting business. Then in the mid-eighties, the PGA Tour became one of my clients. One thing led to another and I found myself down here in Florida as their VP for business operations. The next year I moved to chief operating officer, and five years later, in '94, the board asked me to become commissioner. It's funny—a lot of people assume that my job affords me the opportunity to play a lot of golf, but in truth I only played maybe eight or ten rounds last year. I've got small kids, so between the job and my family, I actually don't play that often. In the future, I'm sure I'll play more, but right now I'm focused on balancing my time between the job and my family.

I think the launch of the First Tee gave me what was probably my best day in golf. It wasn't about me playing golf, but rather being involved with something that I knew would create a whole new generation of golfers. That day we flew around the country with former President Bush, Earl Woods, Tom Watson, and others announcing the program. We started here in Jacksonville and flew to New York, Detroit, and Houston, and people everywhere were enthusiastic about the program. Right off the bat, I noticed a great cross-section of people who had come out to get involved. I remember former President Bush noticed it too, and told me how remarkable it was. Along with all the kids, of course, you had millionaires who love the game and wanted to contribute money; you had people willing to volunteer their time to get the youth programs running and who saw the value of what golf could do for kids in inner cities. And the pros, of course, were really supportive. Tom Watson, for example, had been involved with junior golf in Kansas City, and by virtue of the fact that he was such an articulate speaker in voicing his support, I think Tom gave the program a lot of momentum right from the start.

When you take the long view, however, the most important thing is communicating the greatness of the game to young people everywhere. In our First Tee program, we stress life skills as part of the game very aggressively. The kids we work with learn in such a short period of time so much about the basic elements of life; setting goals, maintaining patience in the face of frustration, playing by the rules and being honest about what you're doing. All those life skills, those core values, are wrapped up in the game of golf, and I think all of us that play recognize it. When you see the young kids today developing those core values, it's very special to see the impact the game can have. Last summer we had a hundred thousand kids go through the First Tee program, so it's safe to say it has really taken off. I am proud that we have the opportunity to make the game more accessible to kids, because if they play early, they are bound to do so later in life. From that perspective, First Tee is awesome.

Having allies in the White House was obviously a great benefit as well. I've had the opportunity to play with former President Bush on several occasions, and he's very humorous and a delightful playing companion. Also, he plays so fast you are hustling to get through the round. He and I were playing in the pro-am one time in Akron at the old World Series of Golf, and he was spraying it a little bit that day, and he pulled his drive on one hole and it just missed this guy lined up on the fairway. The guy yelled: "Mr. President, take it easy. I voted for you!" That same round, on another hole he tried to hit a nine-iron out of the rough, and he pulled it to the other side the fairway and it went right into a garbage can. He said: "That's appropriate. That's exactly where it belongs."

At the end of the day, I think my best days in golf really have everything to do with promoting the sport in my professional capacity and finding ways to present the sport in a relevant way to our fan base. The image of our players in the marketplace enhances our reputation, no question. One of the challenges is making sure we protect that. The presence of guys like Sergio Garcia, Shigeki Maruyama, and K. J. Choi are also very important in bringing the PGA Tour to potential fans in other countries as well.

I love to play the game, too. Since I was a kid, I've managed to play every year on my birthday. In recent years, I've played thirty-six holes with friends at Pablo Creek, a wonderful Tom

Fazio–designed course here in Jacksonville. I think when you're fully engaged and challenged mentally with the game and in a beautiful natural setting, any day on the golf course is a great day. At the Hall of Fame induction this year, Ben Crenshaw quoted Harvey Penick, and said, "A golf course is to me a holy ground. I feel God in the trees, and the grass and the flowers and in the rabbits and in the water. I feel that I am home." As soon as I heard Ben speak those words, I knew it was one of the finest things that has ever been said about the game of golf.

RAYMOND FLOYD

Now a member of the Champions Tour, Raymond Floyd is one of the most tenacious competitors in golf. Among his twenty-two PGA Tour victories, he's won all three American majors, including the PGA Championship twice, and has also piled up thirteen wins on the Champions Tour. He spends a good deal of time these days running his own golf course design firm, a subject he always enjoys talking about.

I grew up on a golf course, so the game was always available to me when I was a kid. My dad was a golf professional— he was the pro at the enlisted men's golf course at Fort Bragg, North Carolina. He got me started at a very early age and taught me the proper way to approach the game. My mom was an influence as well because she was quite a good player, too, so we were a golfing family through and through.

As a young golf fan, Arnold Palmer was my guy, all the way. He was the one winning the tournaments in the late fifties, and he was the King. I watched him play on television at the Masters, and a couple of times my dad took me to the old Azalea Open, which was down in Wilmington, to see the pros perform. After that, it just became my only goal: I wanted to be a touring professional golfer.

There were no two ways about it. I never thought in terms of do I have the ability, or anything like that. Like a lot of kids, I never thought in those terms. I just knew I loved golf, and wanted it to be a big part of my life—doubt or negativity never came into play. I think it's best to set goals as you go along, and when you reach them, that sense of fulfillment is one of the best things in life.

From my standpoint and probably to most professional golfers, as it's been said many times, it's really all about winning the major championships. So when I think of memorable days over my career, I've got to say that the four majors I won on the regular Tour are the ones that stand out without question. There are a fair number of players who win numerous tournaments and never win a major—they won't be Hall of Famers and their careers won't feel that fulfilling. But another player who wins far fewer events but with major titles thrown in the mix—his career will be fulfilling. It takes a kind of discipline to set your sights on the prestigious titles. They're marked on your calendar and you have to direct your practices toward them no matter how you're playing. The Ryder Cup, even though it's a team event, is a lot like the majors in that sense.

But I wouldn't call any of those wins my best day in golf, because to me the heart of the game is something that is shared with friends and family, and I say that even though I made my career from individual success in the game. My best day in golf was winning the first father-son tournament, walking down the last hole with Raymond Jr. while my younger son, Robert, who recently turned pro himself, caddied, and my wife and daughter were in the gallery along with my dad all cheering us on. That meant so much to me. We won over a pretty impressive field of fathers and sons, but that wasn't the point. Just playing and competing together was great, as a matter of family pride. Then winning the tournament again with my son Robert was a dream come true. I think you could poll a lot of players that have competed in these father-son events—Jack Nicklaus, Gary Player, anyone—and they'd all tell you how special it is.

When I got into golf-course design it gave me a whole new perspective on the game, both from a practical standpoint as well as creatively. I realized that I'm a traditionalist at heart. I love the old traditional golf courses. But you've got to know the importance of satisfying a client when you're doing a project. They have ideas or a picture of what they want, so often you are doing something that you might not do if you had total autonomy—though some clients do give you a lot of control.

It's been a great experience studying Donald Ross and McDonald and Tillinghast, after playing their courses, to see the amazing details that era of architects built into their courses. A place like Shinnecock Hills, for example, is truly one of the great golf courses in the world. It's just naturally routed; every hole goes in a different direction. The genius of Shinnecock is in the routing plan. Look at Augusta's routing; same thing. They routed that golf course so that no two holes really run side by side or in the direct, exact direction. It gives a true test to the game over the course of many rounds—mastering it is next to impossible.

Through the years golf has given me a lot of fabulous experiences and I have been fortunate to play with many of the game's greats. If I could play an all-time dream round of golf, I'd want to do it at Augusta, and Arnold Palmer would have to be a part of it. Ben Hogan and Sam Snead would probably fill out the group—I got a chance to play with them later in their careers, and you could tell they both had special skills. It would be fascinating as well to play with some of the guys from earlier eras, like Bobby Jones and Walter Hagen, just to see how their shot making and strategy compared with more modern players. Either way, I'd just hope I could stop admiring those guys long enough to keep my own shots on line.

BILL GADSBY

Hall of Fame defenseman Bill Gadsby manned the blue line for the Chicago Blackhawks, New York Rangers, and Detroit Red Wings during a twenty-year NHL career in which he was a seven-time All-Star. Famous for his reckless, aggressive style of play during an intensely defensive hockey era, Gadsby constantly wore an unending series of battle scars—cuts, bruises, broken noses, and so on. The NHL Hall of Fame points out that Gadsby is one of only a handful of players to have taken out insurance on cuts—though by his reckoning he received at least six hundred stitches to his face,
Gadsby's policy made a lot of sense. At the time of his retirement he was the all-time offensive defenseman. Now in his seventies, he is still extremely active and enjoying retirement. By his count, he played 128 rounds of golf last year, much of it during a six-week trip to Maui. His autobiography, The Grateful Gadsby, *was released in 2003.*

I started playing golf in the mid-fifties, when the game really took off in popularity. I enjoyed it and enjoyed seeing my game improve. The old goalkeeper from the New York Americans, Earl Robertson, introduced me to the game. We went to the driving range together and he gave me a few tips and some encouragement. So I did, and I gained on it every year. Being a professional hockey player I was able to play a lot in the off season and right on through training camp. After practice I used to go out with my Ranger teammates Gump Worsley,

Camille Henry, and Andy Bathgate. In those days I was about a six handicap. It was the lowest I ever got.

Now I'm up to thirteen. As you get older you don't hit it as far or as well. I have a tough time reaching all the par 4s, so I spend a lot of time working on my short game. I am pretty confident that if I am anywhere near the green, I can pitch it up close and make my par. It's amazing to me the number of people that spend all their time hitting drivers and irons, but don't spend enough time on putting and the finesse shots, because that is where you score.

I'd have to say one of my best moments was when I got my hole in one—the only one I ever had—in Edmonton playing with Earl Robertson. It was at Prince Rupert Golf Course, which I don't think is around anymore. The hole was a par 3, about 150 yards straight uphill. I never saw the ball go in the hole, but I knew it was mine because we used to have a connection in Chicago with Wilson, and I was the only person in the group playing the old Wilson K28 ball. When we got up to the green, I knew I'd hit a good shot, but we couldn't find the ball, and we walked around back, looked in the trap behind the green, and then Earl all of a sudden says, "Hey, come over here! You just got a hole in one!" So it was kind of anticlimactic because I didn't know where the hell the ball was, but over the years that memory has gotten better and better. I've been close a lot of times. If you play a lot of golf you're going to get close a few times, but that's like hitting the post in hockey— not quite good enough. I hadn't been playing for very long when I got that ace, but after it happened I never thought it might be my only one. I'm hoping to pick up another in my lifetime.

The other great day was when I had the opportunity to shoot my age. Last summer, I turned seventy-five. I was playing at Western Golf and Country Club. I started out with nine straight 4s on the front side for a 36. It wasn't until the 16th hole that I started thinking about it. I get to the 18th and I needed a par on the last hole to shoot my age. I missed a three-footer for par and shot 76. I normally shoot in the mid-80s so I guess I'll have to wait a few more years before I get a good shot at it.

I still enjoy the game and the camaraderie a lot. I've always enjoyed playing with some of the other guys in the NHL, especially after we all retired from the game. Golf keeps me in contact with former teammates, and the guys I used to knock heads with, now we're all friends. So it's nice to go up to the Hall of Fame tournament at Glen Abbey near Toronto, or the Red Wings charity events where I can BS with some of the younger players like Steve Yzerman and Darren McCarty. I'd say I get maybe eighty charity invites over the course of the year. And Western Golf and Country Club gave me a special membership. I've been there for nine years now, and all they want me to do is play with as many members as I can, so that's another nice perk of my retirement.

Gordie Howe and I used to play quite a bit together. He's a good golfer. I have one funny story about him, though. After the season, our families would go to Florida for a vacation in April. We were playing down there, just him and I one day. He hit his ball close to a canal on the left-hand side of the fairway. I'd hit mine in the same general area but I was 20 yards from the canal. Anyway, Gordie's about five yards from the water, and all of a sudden I see this six-foot snake sitting on the side sunning himself. It made a move toward Gordie, who jumped over to the cart, got his driver out, and tried to smack it. But he missed and the thing slithered back into the water. So we continue playing. About six holes later, he hits his ball near another canal, and as he started to take his stance and address the ball, I snuck up behind him and pinched him right in the back of the leg. (He was wearing Bermuda shorts.) And oh God, he froze for a second, and then took off like a scared rabbit. I was laughing so hard, and he says, "You son of a gun, you rotten scoundrel!" Not a year goes by that we don't remind each other of that story. I got him pretty good.

Another time, in the late sixties, I got Gordie again. We were pretty evenly matched on the golf course, and we always had close matches. One day at Western Golf and Country Club, we were on the last hole, and we're all even. On our second shots, from about 150, I put my ball about 20 feet from the stick and Gordie says, "What did you hit there?"

There was a little wind in our face. I told him I hit an eight-iron. He said, "Wow, it doesn't seem like an eight-iron, but you made a hell of a shot." So he takes out a seven-iron. The way he hit the ball back then he probably should have been playing a nine. Flew the green by 20 yards. His ball landed in the bushes and he didn't have any chance to recover. Gordie says to me again, "What did you hit?"

"Eight-iron."

He says, "Couldn't have been."

I wound up winning the match. I don't think he's ever forgiven me for that. I didn't tell him for three months that I'd actually hit a six-iron. Oh, God, he was angry for a while.

LARRY GATLIN

Larry Gatlin is the leader of the Gatlin Brothers Band. Performing with his brothers Rudy and Steve, they are one of the most popular country music recording artists in history. The Gatlins grew up listening to and singing gospel music, and brought this influence to their inventive country format. Gatlin has scored a number of chart-topping hits both with the trio and as a solo artist, and he still hits the road from time to time, as well as performing with his brothers at their theater in Branson, Missouri.

ut in West Texas, where I'm from, football was king, so I didn't play much golf when I was growing up. I picked it up when I was in college. I went to the University of Houston on a football scholarship, and lived in the athletic dorm with a lot of the golfers. At that time, UH had won something like twelve NCAA titles and had dominated college golf for years with their famous coach, Dave Williams. So many players have come from there—Fuzzy Zoeller, Fred Couples, Hal Underwood, and of course, John Mahaffey, who is a great friend of mine from those years.

The next series of events that really got me into the game was after we moved to Nashville and made a couple of hit records. People started inviting us to play pro-ams. The very first one I went to was the Greater Greensboro Open, where I played with John Mahaffey. I hadn't seen John in four or five years, but by then he had become one of the best players out on the tour. And I've just played a lot ever since.

But my very best day in golf came while I was on tour starring as the Confederate captain in Frank Wildhorn's great musical, *The Civil War*. We had Monday off in Atlanta, and Charlie Yates, Jr. invited me, and my son Josh, to play with him at Augusta National. I was even par through six holes, but it was a greater joy to watch my son, who's a two handicap, get to play that sacred and hallowed course. That, to me, transcended golf. It was about friendship and family and the honor of the game itself. And to watch Josh shoot 75 from the back tees at Augusta was my best day in golf. I came back about eight months later and shot 73 from the middle tees, but it was just a true pleasure to provide that memory for my son. Charles Yates took a picture of Josh standing at Amen Corner. For my birthday Josh took that picture and had it framed, and the caption underneath just says: "Amen, brother, Amen." He's a wonderful young man.

You can pick any emotion and I can associate it with a golf memory, that's how much the game is a part of my life. Meeting Arnold Palmer at the Gatlin Brothers Senior tournament, and playing for charity with him. That's respect. Playing with Crenshaw, Jack Nicklaus, both President Bushes. Meeting Ben Hogan. I admire all of them so much. Watching my friends, like Crenshaw, Tom Kite, and Curtis Strange, win majors and how much it means to them—I get as much pleasure from watching that as playing myself. Pride. Singing the national anthem at the Ryder Cup the year the Americans made that amazing comeback, winning nine matches on the final day.

And then there's the tragedy of life too. My dear friend Jay O'Neill was staying at our house here in Austin, and on September 11, 2001 my guitar player, Steve Smith, called me first thing and said: "Larry, you got to get up and look. Somebody's crashed a plane into the World Trade towers." I went and woke Jay up and we all watched in disbelief as the second plane hit the tower, and watched them crumble. Finally, after watching from eight o'clock in the morning until three o'clock in the afternoon, I said: "Jay, I can't take any more of this, I really can't.

This may seem horrible, but let's go play nine holes of golf. I got to get outside. I feel like I'm smothered in here, and need to clear my mind." We'd sat in front of the TV for seven hours, so we went out and played, but we weren't thinking about golf. After every shot, we'd come back to the cart: "What are we going to do? What's America going to do? Are we going to bounce back? You think there are other things on the way?" In the first tee box, we prayed for the people who had been killed—God, help their families. Our hearts went out to them. I went out, and because I wasn't thinking about golf, I shot 69, the best score I've ever shot in my life on the most tragic day in American history since Fort Sumter. So my personal best day in golf is actually one of my worst memories.

But on the flip side, I think of all the great laughs I've had on the golf course. A few years ago, Steve and Rudy and I went to Palm Springs, and one of us had the idea to do a little video to open our shows and show the brothers, playing golf. Ernie Vossler of Landmark Country Club gave us the run of the course for a couple of days to shoot our golf video. We came up with a little story. Normally Rudy beats us, so this time Steve and I would be beating him. But at every opportunity, Rudy would run up and knock the ball in the rough, or step on the ball so it was in a divot, or throw it in the sand, just basically cheating to win. We were going to speed up the film to make it a funny, Keystone Cops kind of thing. At the end, we were going to catch Rudy cheating and tie him to a tree and leave him there.

So we worked on it for about three days, and got to the last scene. We tied Rudy up with a hose, and he started wiggling and squirming, trying to free himself, and we just let the camera roll. All of a sudden, Rudy started screaming and hollering and cussing at us and saying awful words that we knew we couldn't use on that video.

We had tied the boy up in a bed of fire ants. We realized something was wrong and we untied him. He had to take every stitch of clothing off, and he was running around, Steve and I hitting him with our shirts and caps, laughing hysterically. That's the way brothers are. He was absolutely eaten up. That's the funniest thing I've ever seen on the golf course. Later, we reshot the last scene, but we used it to open our shows, and people loved it.

Here's what I've learned from golf—we made a funny video out of it, but everyone knows it's true. I've learned that if a man would cheat you on the golf course, he'll cheat you in business. Don't do business with him. If you're playing the ball down, play the damn ball down. If the fairway's not in good shape and everybody's going to roll it over, that's fine too, as long as everybody plays the same rules, you know? But I've played with men who are very well-to-do and some of them cheat. I don't care to have that much money, thank God. But I remember not that long ago, my friend Bill Nunn was being interviewed, and he was asked about George W. Bush, who is a friend of ours. And the interviewer said, "You've been a friend of the president's for a long time. Tell me what you think about him." And Bill said very simply: "He doesn't move his ball, he doesn't move his ball, he doesn't cheat." That says it all right there. I'm looking forward to playing with him again next time he has some time down in Texas.

I've won a Grammy Award and became a member of the Grand Ole Opry. I've sung in Carnegie Hall and the Palace Theatre, so music has really given me so much in life. But having the opportunity to play golf with so many great Americans is one of the best by-products of my music career. I'm poor oil-field trash from Odessa, Texas, and I wouldn't have had those opportunities if not for music. So many gracious, generous people have given me these memories, and with my own charity events, I've tried my best to pass the joys of golf on to others.

ROD GILBERT

Legendary New York Rangers right wing Rod Gilbert, like many hockey pros, made a smooth transition from the rink to the links, and counts golf as one of his favorite pastimes. Elected to the Hockey Hall of Fame in 1982 after eighteen sterling seasons with the Rangers, the Montreal native finished his career with 406 goals and 1,021 total points.

In the NHL, our off season is during the summer, so golf is a natural hobby for a lot of players. I learned on a municipal course in Montreal, but even during the season I thought about golf a fair amount. All those years my roommate was Jean Ratelle, and on road trips we would practice in our hotel room. We had Ben Hogan's *Fundamentals of Golf*—the "five easy lessons"—and that was the only book we used. Jean and I used to take hockey sticks and practice the grip, the shoulder turn, and the "triangle," and that's how we learned. Then, in the off season, I would play with some of the club pros around Montreal and practice what I learned.

When I think of my favorite golf stories, it seems that Jean Lapointe plays a part in a lot of them. For those who don't know that much about Quebec, Lapointe was a very famous singer with the duo Les Jerolas. They were the first Quebecois performers to appear on *The Ed Sullivan Show*. He's a senator now, in Prime Minister Chrétien's government. Anyway, Lapointe loved a friendly wager now and then, and he's an avid golfer. I'm not a gambling man, but Lapointe always thought that his game was a little better than it actually was, and he'd seek me out. In those days, a hockey player's salary wasn't even close to what it is now, and Lapointe was making at least $500,000 a year, so he had a lot on the side, and I didn't feel bad about beating him. He said he was a 14 handicap, but he was more like a 22. He was an erratic player, but such a good gambler that he could put on enough pressure that I'd miss a three-foot putt and choke like a dog. Again, I had a lot more to lose than him, so the times when I lost weighed on me. I started not to really like the game for the game itself—but that was just a passing phase.

Well, my best day in golf happened in a foursome with Lapointe, Jean Cloutier, and Yvon "The Roadrunner" Cournoyer of the Montreal Canadiens. On the 17th hole, I was up eight hundred dollars and Lapointe placed a bet—two hundred and two hundred for the last two holes—you'd have to win match and medal. So I accepted, and on the 17th, a par-3, I thought I saw my friend with a nine-iron in his hand. It was actually a six-, but I was looking at it upside down! Well, I was a little nervous, seeing him only reach the front of the green with that club. I hit a six as well, and of course I flew the green. As soon as I hit it I remembered the deep ravine behind the green, and thought my day was over. But there was also a huge, tall oak tree just to the left, and my ball hit the top branch—maybe 150 yards away. The ball caromed off the tree, dropped on the green, and rolled in the hole. I had a hole in one! It's my only one—after playing for forty years, I'm still looking for my second.

Lapointe fell over backward, and he couldn't breathe for a while. He was in total shock. I was laughing so hard—I couldn't believe it. And that was the last time I ever played for money with him. You have to quit while you're ahead.

One of the funniest memories I have is of one of my Rangers teammates, Jim Neilson. Jim was a full Creole Indian from Saskatchewan. He'd never played golf in his life. The Rangers sponsored a golf tournament every year, which would give you the day off. But you had to skate if you didn't play golf that day. So Jim says: "I play golf."

I said: "Jimmy, you don't play golf."

"Today I do."

At the tournament we rented him some clubs and I told him to buy some cheap balls, three for a dollar. He bought six balls. Guess what? Lost them all on the first hole. So I gave him three of mine, Titleists, the good ones. He loses those. By the turn I must have given him a dozen balls, and I pointed to the pro shop and said: "You want to play some more?"

"Yeah, I'm getting better."

Well, he went to the pro shop, but didn't actually buy anything! And while I was on the tee, he went into my bag and stole a few more! I wasn't pleased. I said: "What happened to the balls you bought?"

"If you can't afford the game, don't play it."

I shrugged it off, but I decided to get him for that little remark. Somewhere on the back nine one of my drives went off course and into the edge of the woods. It was September, so I took a club and was moving leaves aside, searching for my ball, when I saw something move—it was a little field snake. I jumped after the snake and trapped it, wrapping it around my club. Then I went back to my bag and put it in the pocket where I kept the golf balls.

On the very next tee, Jim starts fishing around in my bag. But he's watching me, to see if I'm aware of what he's doing, not looking in the bag. Suddenly his hand came out.

"Jesus!"

And the snake was wrapped around his wrist! Well, that was a shocker for him. I said: "Don't take my balls anymore." Not that that was an issue. I don't think Jim ever played golf from that day on.

BRYANT GUMBEL

Bryant Gumbel has a distinguished broadcasting career spanning four decades, and his versatility has allowed him to move easily between sports and news journalism. Beginning his broadcast career in Los Angeles in 1972, Gumbel quickly became NBC's lead anchor for the NFL, NCAA basketball, and Major League Baseball games. In 1982, he was named anchor of The Today Show, *a post he would hold for the next fifteen years. Currently, he hosts the award-winning HBO series* Real Sports with Bryant Gumbel. *One look at the seven-handicapper's Manhattan office, practically overflowing with golf memorabilia, is all one needs to understand his passion for the game.*

I got into golf quite by accident, actually. I didn't take it up until I was about thirty years old. My dad had played in Chicago when I was growing up, but it wasn't something that really interested me then. So I became one of those guys who went around playing just once a year, never really improving. Then one day, on the last hole of my "annual" round, I hit the perfect shot, a five-iron—it had the perfect trajectory, sat down right where I aimed it, and I had no idea how it happened. I was off that week, so I decided to go back the next day, see if I could figure out why it happened, and I'm still searching. That's what keeps you coming back, that rare perfect shot.

Today, I've gotten to the point where I generally hit the ball pretty straight, but I don't have a glamorous game. I'm not long, but I am consistent, so even when I play lousy, I can go out there and know I'll have a fairly decent round.

I'd say my best day in golf was in 1994, when I was Johnny Miller's playing partner at the AT&T Pebble Beach National Pro-Am, which was his last victory on the PGA Tour. I'd played with Johnny for several years before that, but playing Pebble Beach in the final group of a PGA Tour tournament is easily the best experience an amateur like me could ever have in the game. If you want to hear frightening words before you step to the first tee, have somebody over the loudspeaker at Pebble Beach say, "Ladies and gentlemen, and now our final foursome, playing with the co-leaders . . ."

In terms of talent, I'm not even in the top half of the amateur field, but I've had an odd way of making most of the cuts. The way I grind it out on the course helps somewhat, and that's how it was that year. The first day we didn't exactly set the world on fire—if you'll remember, Johnny's winning score for the tournament was something like seven under. But on the second day I looked at the leaderboard and saw we were five under as a team, and I said, "Isn't that something, as bad as we've played, we're right there." Johnny said, "Let's just have a good time." The galleries were cheering for him, because he's from the Bay Area, and I told him he'd be a really popular winner. "No, we don't have a chance," he modestly replied.

Johnny hadn't won a tournament in almost ten years, so he was really just playing for fun. He didn't even have a full bag, to be honest. He had a driver, a seven-wood, and a handful of other clubs, and he never really thought he had a shot at it until the final day. Johnny's putting stroke deserted him years ago, but he is such a pure striker of the ball it's frightening. It was amazing to watch him competing against Tom Watson that year, because the contrast between their games is like night and day. Johnny had said he was always unnerved by the idea of going up against Watson, because he always felt that Tom could drain a 30-footer for birdie.

I'll never forget that Sunday, when we reached the 17th, and the two were tied. As we waited on the tee we watched Tom three-putt, and suddenly Johnny was the leader with two holes to play. The pin was in the back left, Sunday placement, and the wind was howling off the ocean. The hole must have been playing 215 yards, about 30 to 40 yards longer than normal. I turned to Johnny and said, "What are you going to hit?" he said, "I don't know. You hit." I stepped up with a three-wood, and hit it dead on the screws.

Within a second after hitting it, the crowd went *berserk*. And in the stands, they started going "We're not worthy, we're not worthy!" Although I don't see well, I knew it hadn't been gone long enough to be an ace, so I had no idea what was going on. The first person I caught sight of was Gary McCord. And Gary goes, "You hit a gull." Evidently, a seagull was coming off the ocean, and I hit it right in the coconut. He knocked the ball 50 yards right, out of bounds, and the seagull fell deader than disco. I just killed it, flat on the spot. It was so bad: Some guy ran out there and grabbed the poor dead critter by the neck and held it up like this, and started screaming at the crowd. I was mortified! To this day, when I go back to Pebble I always hear some wannabe comic screaming, "Hey, Bryant, gonna kill a bird today?" I have to remind people it's not like I hooked the ball into a bird sanctuary. I hit it right down the middle, and the poor creature was coming off the ocean, and it was the last thing he ever did. Dave Winfield would know what I'm talking about.

Then it was Johnny's turn. Most pros were hitting two-irons and three-irons that day. But he didn't have those clubs, so for him the only option was a four-iron, which he took out and somehow managed to eke onto the front of the green, from where he two-putted. So now we go to the signature hole, the par-5 18th, with a one-stroke lead. He reached the green in regulation, and as we walked up to the green I wanted to say: "Johnny, when you putt out, can I have the ball?" But I didn't want to freak him out, because Johnny putting out is never a guarantee. So I said nothing. Wouldn't you know it, as soon as he knocked it in he reached into the cup, took the ball, and threw it in the ocean! Even though I didn't get the ball, my favorite moment of the day was when they presented the check. The first thing Johnny said was: "I want to thank my playing partner, Bryant Gumbel." It brought a lump to my throat.

On a day-to-day basis, my best days in golf come from playing with my buddies at The Whippoorwill Club just outside New York City. The course is a classic Donald Ross design and it's just fun. And, of course, the rounds I play with Matt Lauer are always great. The funny thing is although we're best friends, Matt is one of the more noncompetitive golfers I've ever played with, which is odd, because I'm just the opposite. He wants to win, but he doesn't want to know during the round who's getting a stroke, where we stand, or anything else. It's just the strangest thing, because even if I don't want to know, I always *know.* That's why I'm always amused when these magazines say, "Try not to keep score." How can you not? I don't know any golfers who need paper and pencil, to tell many fairways, how many greens, how many putts, and so on. Invariably, Matt and I shoot virtually the exact same score every time out. Matt's longer than I am; I'm much more consistent than he is. He's a much better iron player; I'm a much better putter. We always play even.

One of the best memories we share was the day we played against two guys, both in the golf business, down at St. Andrews at Grand Cypress in Orlando, Florida. It was a rainy day. On the 15th hole, one of our opponents hit his approach shot onto the green, but it was about 95 feet away—because it's a links-style course, with contiguous double greens. The putt had multiple breaks and was impossible to read. Anyway this guy made a full turn and hit the ball, and it was moving all over the place when . . . *bang!* It goes in. We all fall down laughing, screaming—it was one of the longest putts anyone had ever made, anywhere, anytime. When we finally settled down, it was my turn and I had about a 70-footer myself, also an impossible putt. But miracle of miracles I banged it in right behind him for another birdie. It was amazing—two putts drained from a total of about 165 feet. We just laughed and laughed and laughed. Those were two of the most improbable putts. We wound up beating the two "pros" pretty badly. One of the guys actually didn't have the money to pay us. He was embarrassed. He asked us where we were having dinner that night, and he actually showed up that night at the restaurant and paid us. It was admirable, but not surprising—because win or lose, the game's about honor and you can't say that about any other sport.

BOB HOPE

Other than PGA Tour pros, it's hard to imagine any celebrity as inexorably tied to the game of golf as Bob Hope. At age 100, he is older than most of the courses he has played on. Hope says he's played on over two thousand courses around the world.

I like to tell myself that my best day in golf was the second time I tried it. That was in the spring of 1930—when the only people who made real money from the game were chiropractors. I had tried golf in 1927 in Cleveland, where, incidentally, I'd grown up, and I just had no feel for the game. I had never taken lessons and I was terrible.

Anyway, I was in vaudeville playing the Orpheus circuit, the northern route, doing afternoon and evening shows in Winnipeg, Calgary, Minneapolis, Seattle, and Tacoma. I used to do four shows a day in vaudeville, great for your self-confidence, then drop into a nightclub. I might do thirty or forty minutes off the cuff. I thought nothing of working from twelve to one o'clock the next day. I'd make a line seem like nothing; it's the opposite of hitting a joke too hard.

But there wasn't much to do in the morning before twelve, except maybe sit around the lobby of the hotel and drink coffee. On the circuit with me were the Diamond Brothers, a comedy act. They always traveled with their golf clubs and played every morning.

They always asked me to join them for a round, I finally decided that it had to be better than sitting forever in that dreary hotel lobby. So one day I borrowed a set of clubs. I hit a bag of practice balls and played a few holes. I've been in love with the game ever since. In fact, I consider golf my profession, and comedy just a way to pay my green fees.

I guess I've played golf on more than two thousand courses from Brazil to Bangkok and in the company of some of the greatest people on earth—other golfers. I've had seven holes in one, but at my age and playing as many rounds as I have that shouldn't be too surprising. So when I'm asked, "What is your best golf story, or your best day on the golf course?" the truth is I'm stumped for an answer. There have been so many great moments that it's impossible to say, "Oh, I remember, it was here."

On the other hand, there are some golf matches I'd like to forget. But for some reason or another, people, lots of them, won't let me. Like the day I was partnered with my wife Delores at a couples' match in Palm Springs. At the end of 18 holes, the announcer gave the scores—Bob Hope, 78, Delores Hope, 76.

It's amazing how much frustration and how much fun can come from following a little white ball around all day. Sometimes the fun can be traced to where I was playing, or how I was playing. Most of the time it came because of who was in the foursome. The really great days occurred when these things all came together.

Someone once irreverently suggested that Palm Springs is where God would live and play if He had the money. I wouldn't go that far, but I must admit I've had some genuinely wonderful times and played to some great crowds in my many visits to Palm Springs. On almost every visit, photographer Bob Davidoff was there, temporarily blinding me with his strobe. And if it wasn't me, Bob was ready with that camera for just about any newsworthy resident or visitor. One of my many prized golf photographs is from President Ford. It's autographed and reads, "I'll try to get better next time." Another was taken on the day I beat President Eisenhower. I did it without cheating, which is hard to do with the Secret Service constantly looking over your shoulder. Politicians are pretty good golfers—they're terrific when they get around the green.

We had some fun with President Ford on one such visit. By the way, I love playing with Jerry Ford. If you beat him, he pardons you. President Ford was giving a speech at a Palm Beach convention; he began by saying, "Lots of people think I'm a lousy golfer. That's not so. Bob Hope has been spreading this rumor all over the country. Actually, I'm a very good golfer." Of course, Jerry then gives you five or ten minutes, maybe more, on just how good he is. Oh, well, it gets laughs, even though I thought we'd had a deal—he governed, I got the laughs.

Next day, Bob Davidoff sets up to photograph President Ford during a round of golf. The Secret Service told Bob, "Get behind the golf cart, get behind the tree. Don't distract him." As Bob tells it, Ford was three feet from the cup, and his playing partner wanted it called a "gimme." But Jerry insisted on putting out. After circling or stalking the putt for several minutes, he yipped it.

I'm in town a few weeks later, and Bob calls and tells me he has a picture of Ford lining up his putt, and that he missed it. The result is my loving note, written on the photograph. "To President Ford—I always wait, too." To this day, Jerry Ford insists that was his birdie shot, and that he'd just missed an eagle putt. Davidoff says it was Ford's sixth shot on a par-5. We might have called the congressional committee and ask for a hearing to straighten out that one. Just kidding. There is no finer guy, in or out of politics, than Jerry Ford. To me, it was a gimme.

GORDIE HOWE

"Mr. Hockey," Gordie Howe is simply the greatest hockey player to ever play the game. He hardly needs any introduction for fans of the sport, but for those unfamiliar with Canada's national game, his statistics speak for themselves. At the time of his retirement at age fifty-two, after playing professionally for thirty-two years, he held more records than anyone else in team sports history. Entering the NHL with the Detroit Red Wings in 1946 at the age of eighteen, number 9 posted all-time records for goals, assists, points, games played, scoring titles, and All-Star appearances. Mr. Hockey won seven MVP awards, and was the foundation of the Production Line—the Red Wings machine of the 1950s that won seven NHL titles to rank among the greatest sports dynasties ever. 2003 marks the golden anniversary of Mr. Hockey's marriage to Mrs. Hockey, Colleen Howe.

I started playing golf when I was fourteen years old. I used to hunt for golf balls, searching the bushes on the city course in Saskatoon. The ones that weren't scuffed up too badly I'd resell. Pat Fletcher was the pro and he didn't mind, he just told me to stay off the fairways. So one day I was out looking for balls and I found a club in there—I believe it was a five-iron. And I started out playing with just that one club. As a teenager I used to practice in the backyard, and there was a lot of room out there. By that time, I'd also found a three-iron, so I'd practice with both of them. There was a home across the way that had a couple of horses and a barn. I would aim at the barn, and I got to the point where I could smack the ball pretty dang good.

I remember one day my dad came along, and he was quite an athlete in his day. He says, "What are you doing?"

"I was just hitting some golf balls."

"Here. Let me show you how." He takes my club, winds up, and takes a huge cut at the ball. "Where'd it go?" he said.

I said, "It's still on the tee."

Then he throws the club down and says, "Go play your stupid golf." I just started laughing.

I finally tried to give it a go on a real course, and I shot in the low eighties the first time out. I had no idea how tough the game really was. But I think hockey helped my swing tremendously. I didn't realize it at the time, but you're working on a similar motion, and everything needs to be square at impact, like when you're shooting a hockey puck, too. Having the slap shot ingrained in my muscle memory was a good starting point.

It took me a little while to get good enough, where I could compete on a serious level. I got down to scratch and entered the Canadian Open, the big amateur tournament, when I was about twenty-one. Pat Fletcher, the pro from the City Course I mentioned before, helped enter me in the tournament—he was a real nice guy and a big hockey fan. I won my first match, and I was feeling pretty good because there wasn't a hole on the course I couldn't reach in two. In the second round I lost on a technicality. In that round, there was a 240-yard par-3, a long hole. I hit my drive into the greenside trap, and when I approached my ball I'll be damned if I didn't turn my ankle and fall down in the trap. The scorekeeper was watching and called the hole on me for testing the sand. Testing the sand . . . I ate it. The guy felt terrible about the call, but that was the rule. I said I didn't mind, but, being that young, I lost my cool inside. I got so mad I blew one out of bounds on the next hole. I wound up losing two and one, which wasn't bad, but I shouldn't have let the technicalities bother me. Maturity in golf takes a long time to develop. From that point on I didn't really enjoy the pressures of tournament golf that much. I decided to stick with a pro career in hockey.

There were other things about that event that are better memories. Meeting Moe Norman was one of them—he could really smoke the ball. He was hard to talk to, but he took a liking to me. I was having a little trouble with the putting stroke and he took me aside and said, "Your stroke is too loose. Just crank in your wrists a little bit." So he showed me, and had me freeze in the position he was talking about, and after that I started putting like a demon.

One of the best rounds I ever had, many years ago, also gave me one of the worst guilty feelings I can remember. There was a young man whose father offered to give me new equipment as a present if I scored a hat trick in the next game, because my mother couldn't afford them. Mr. Rolley Howes was the father's name—he liked me for some reason, and I didn't want to disappoint him so I scored the hat trick and added six assists as well. Anyway, his son was about my age, and he was a pretty good golfer, but he was extremely high-strung—he'd spent some time in the hospital off and on to rest up.

One day Mr. Howes arranged for us to play a match at Waskesiu Golf Course. So we went out, and at the end of nine holes, I had him down by nine. I beat him 10 and 8, and after that 10th hole he just dropped his clubs and sat down. I said to myself: *Oh, God, what have I done?* I couldn't hit a bad shot if I tried that day. I approached him and said, "Hey, I'm very sorry for what happened, but I'm extremely happy for my game and I'm sorry you weren't on yours." I really hoped I wasn't sending him back for another stretch at the sanitarium. I think he had only about three pars, and I birdied everything he parred. I wasn't even thinking about it until I looked at the card and realized the match was over. I didn't want to embarrass him too much in front of friends, so I suggested we play until the 15th or 16th hole, and at that point he called the match, picked up my ball, and shook my hand.

As a professional hockey player I have been fortunate to meet many great people. A lot of them were on the golf course. I have played with the likes of Lee Trevino, Chi Chi Rodriguez, and Sam Snead. I also enjoy playing with my sons Mark and Marty, when I can drag them out on the course. One day Mark and I were playing at River Oaks, when I hit a shot to the edge of the lake. I went over to look for my ball in the high weeds.

Mark said: "Dad, don't go, there are a bunch snakes in there."

I must have found about twenty balls in there. As I was picking up the balls, something stirred, and this little snake, no more than three or four feet, was sitting up there looking at me.

I said, "Mark, throw me the driver."

He said, "Dad, get out of there."

I said, "No, just give me the driver." He'd scared me and I was mad.

Mark yelled, "Dad, he's right behind you!"

I hit him on the head and that sucker was mad. He came out of the bush about chest high in a straight line looking at me about three feet away. I got my butt out of there in a hurry. You know, that snake screwed up my whole game. I was shaking for the next three holes.

Another memorable round I had was early in my hockey career, when I was only making about $8,000 a year. A local businessman (I'd rather not say his name) approached me and invited me to a tournament he was involved with. After the event, we had a bite to eat, then went with a couple of friends to have a friendly game at Lake Point, on the east side of Detroit. So I agreed. He was this little Italian guy, and one of the first things I noticed was that he had really nice swing. I started wondering what his handicap was, and I asked the other guys but they didn't know. The fellow says, "We'll just make a little bet, we'll play two for the front, two for the back and two for the match." And I'm thinking, *Okay, two dollars—it's not going to break me.*

So we started playing, and my partner and I were 1 up going to the 9th hole, and the man says, "We're pressing." And we won that hole, too. They press again, we win again, and we got on a streak. I'm thinking we're into these guys for around twenty dollars. But the guy's getting a little mad, saying we're greedy, money-hungry sandbaggers, giving us all kinds of crap. I told my partner, Ed, "I can't wait till this game's over so I can tell him to shove his clubs where they belong."

On the last hole, a par-5, he presses one more time. I was on the green in two, had about a 10-foot putt for eagle. Well, I missed it, but tapped in for birdie to win another hole. Now I'm really getting livid with my opponent's behavior. I said, "Damn, your lumber company must be in bad shape if you can't afford a sixty-dollar debt. You ought to have somebody come over and do your banking for you."

He says: "Who said sixty? It was two hundred, two hundred, two hundred."

I looked at him and replied: "Why the hell didn't you tell me that on the first tee? I'd have walked home." I don't bet that kind of money, and I'd love to know if he would've tried to settle that kind of account with me if he had actually won. He took all the fun out of what had been a good game. But I wouldn't take his money. I was furious. I said, "Don't put your hands in your pocket, either. I wouldn't take a nickel from you!" I didn't even take a shower. I had the clubs sent straight to my car and got the hell out of there as quick as I could.

The funny part is that I saw this businessman well beyond that time. Toward the end of the next season, I was out with my fiancée, Colleen, and we ran into this guy. I introduced them and he said, "Oh, any plans for you guys?" I told him that yeah, in fact, we were going to get married at the end of the season and go on our honeymoon. He asked where we were going, and I told him Fort Lauderdale. Then he said, "Give me a second," and he goes off for a little while. When he came back, he told us that he had gotten us a beautiful suite of rooms a half block from the beach, for three weeks. And we took him up on it. I said, "God, I can't thank you enough for this."

"There's nothing I could do," he told me, "to take away that bad taste I had in my mouth when you told me to keep my hands out of my pockets. This is a way of saying thank you." So that awful round had a happy ending. Golf is a very honorable sport, and people pay their debts somewhere down the road or they do something nice for you, and I think that's one of the great things about the game. Obviously, this guy had been thinking about that day for a long time and was glad to have it off his conscience. To this day, the more things I do with this guy, the nicer he becomes.

BRUCE JENNER

At the 1976 Olympic Games in Montreal, Bruce Jenner shattered the decathlon world record, winning the gold medal and earning the title of the World's Greatest Athlete. Since then, the determination and energy Jenner needed to win the gold has splintered off in many directions—he still loves to test himself in many different aspects in life. The list of hats worn by Bruce Jenner are numerous, among them: devoted father of ten; author; TV commentator; entrepeneur; motivational speaker; pilot; race-car driver; and serious amateur golfer working his way down to scratch.

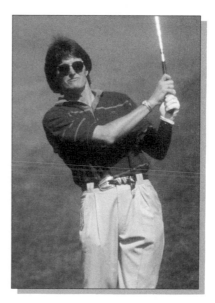

When I was training for the Olympics, I took up golf because it was the only sport I could do outside of training where I didn't have to worry about injuring myself. I never took it seriously, just played once or twice a month with friends, and that was about the extent of it for the next twenty-five years. I always knew it was the type of game that you have to really work at to get good. So I just hacked around, but I always knew that at some point in my life I would like to play the game well. I just didn't know when that would be.

Well, when I hit the big 5-0, my wife told me, "This is a big birthday for you. I've got a few things in mind. I can throw you a big party, or buy you a nice gift, but there's one other thing I would like to do for you that is very special. It would change your life, but for that to happen, there will be things going across your desk that you'll have to sign that you don't know what you're signing. You've got twenty-four hours to think about it."

Now, I know my wife has always done really well in the present department, so I had to put a little faith in her. Needless to say, at one point I get these papers, everything's blocked out but my signature, and I have to sign them. Right before my birthday, she blindfolded me and put me in the car and drove me somewhere. We got out of the car and I heard the voices of a few of my friends, and the group was walking me around. When they took off the blindfold I was at Sherwood Country Club—the nicest place you could ever want to be a member.

I was thrilled. I told her how happy I was, how you couldn't possibly find a better club. Then I told her the bad news. "You just lost your painter, your fix-it guy, your car-pool guy, because you'll know where to find me. I'm seriously going to start working on this game." Three weeks after joining, they had their club championships, so I went in for three days of medal play, everything in the cup, and shot 98, 98, 101. I was pretty humbled by that, finished third from last, and at that point I knew I had a lot of work to do.

Now, three years later, I'm getting pretty close to scratch. But it has taken a lot of work. With the exception of a few lessons from the Sherwood pro, I taught myself. I put in a lot of hard work, hitting tons of balls, reading books and experimenting. It hasn't been really until the last couple of months that I've actually kind of felt like a golfer. When you come from the "real world" of athletics, aggression is good. You get psyched up, you throw that shot far, baby, just get behind that sucker and channel that aggression. But in this game, you get aggressive, you're a dead man. That was probably the hardest thing to get over, learning how not to be aggressive under pressure. You need to pick your spots to go for it. The driver's the only club in the bag where you try to hit it really far. All the others you try to hit a specific distance.

After my first year at Sherwood, I decided to play in my first Celebrity Players Tour tournament in Lake Tahoe. I wasn't ready yet, but I just wanted to see what it was like. I had been thinking about that day for a long time—what it would be like to play competitively in front of all the cameras and people in the crowd. When the day came, I was warming up at the driving range, hitting my four-wood off the tee. Overall, I was pretty pleased and felt confident I'd be able to get off that first tee.

But as soon as I walked out onto the tee box, my heart started pounding. I realized how crazy it was and I was thinking to myself, *God, this is horrible. Why are you doing this?* Then the announcer comes over the PA and says, "Ladies and gentlemen, Bruce Jenner, the world's greatest athlete."

Great introduction—but that was the last thing I needed to hear at that moment—exactly *not* what I needed to calm those butterflies down. Anyway, I turned to the people in the grandstand and made an announcement of my own. I said, "Hey, ladies and gentlemen, here's the deal. This is the first tournament I've ever played in. All of a sudden when I got up here, my heart's been pounding and the adrenaline is really flowing. As all of you know, that's not a good sign. So this is what's going to happen. I'm going to try to hit that ball. If I just make contact, it will be a major accomplishment and I would like polite applause. But if I smack it right down the middle, give me thunderous applause and get me off and on my way, 'cause I'll have overcome a lot."

So now all people in the stands are saying stuff like, "All right, Bruce. Hey, we're right behind you."

I thought that might help take the edge off a bit, but it didn't work. I got over the ball, looked down the fairway, then topped it and the ball rolled a hundred feet.

The crowd gave polite applause. I thanked them and said I knew I was going to be in trouble. Everyone laughed, and on my second shot I hit a tree limb and the ball came straight down. Anyway, I double-bogeyed the first hole. After that, I played pretty well once that first hole was out of the way and I had a really good time.

After the front nine I'd relaxed, and I took out my driver on the 10th tee, which is right next to number 1. This time I smacked it right down the middle, and I got this wild applause—

a standing ovation—from the first tee. It was really funny, because the people on my tee had no idea what the big deal was, but the people on the first tee who had seen my topped shot knew the story and helped me out. So I gave a big bow to the other tee and continued on my way.

My goal for the years to come is to try to crack the top ten on the Celebrity Players Tour. That's kind of my mission. The way I see it, there are four or five guys out there who are trying to win the tournament, the Rick Rhodens and Dan Quinns. Those guys have played competitive golf all their life. They're going to shoot anywhere from five to eight under in 36 holes. I mean, they'll eat the course alive. They're tough to beat. Then you've got that next group that took it up after their career and are more or less scratch players. The quarterbacks Steve Bartkowski and Mark Rypien fall into this category. They'll give the big boys a run for their money, but it's tough for them over 36 holes to consistently play with those guys. And then there's everyone else—the rest of the field is going to shoot between 74 and 79. And that's at least half the field. So my mission is to try to just get past those guys where I can get into the top ten, but I've got to shoot pretty close to scratch to do that and they're all really good athletes as well. I'm kind of right in the middle of the pack right now, but this year if I keep practicing I think I can make that next jump. My game's improved a lot. So I guess you could say I'm in training for my best day in golf.

MATT LAUER

Matt Lauer, the host of NBC's
Today, *considers himself*
a serious golfer. When he is not
interviewing a head of state, he
can be found playing with and
against many of the biggest stars
in Hollywood and the sports world.

When I'm playing golf with a couple of buddies, I get the feeling it's like going home. There's a natural affection, because somewhere in the weird nerve ending in the back of your brain, something's spiraling off memories of those days when you're ten years old, spending four hours with your hero, who's your father. And so why wouldn't you still get this incredibly calm, peaceful feeling when you walk on a golf course?

There was a time when I used to be able to get out and play golf two, three times a week. But the job I have with the *Today* show isn't conducive to that. I have to arrive at the NBC studios a little before five each morning, and, except on Fridays, when I tend to sneak out early, I usually leave at two thirty in the afternoon. So it's a long day. Now having said that, if I decide one day a week that I want to go out and play golf, I'll just move everything off that day, and I can be on the course in

Greenwich at probably eleven that morning. So I'll play that afternoon and just do twice the amount of work the next day.

I sometimes think that the best thing about my job is the access it gives me to great golf. Bryant Gumbel and I play a lot together and we talk about our terrific access all the time. We've been invited to play golf at courses most people only dream of playing. We've played Pebble Beach, Augusta, everywhere that you read about or watch on TV. I've been invited to play with great pros, wonderful celebrities, and with people who run the courses. It's an amazing privilege. I find I sometimes stand in the middle of a round and stop and think I should really pinch myself.

One time, Bryant and I went down to Augusta National. We were invited by Jack Welch, the former chairman of General Electric, and Bob Wright, who's chairman and CEO of NBC. Anyway, Bryant and I checked into one of the cottages at Augusta. It was two weeks before the Masters, so the course was being whipped into serious shape. The greens were rolling. We had the best caddies in the place. And there I was, walking down a fairway on a course I've seen a hundred times on television and I'm remembering who blew a putt from what position, and it was like playing golf and living golf at the same time.

That particular day, it was Bryant and me against Jack Welch and Bob Wright. Jack's about a four handicap. Bob Wright's not quite as low, but he loves the game. Bryant and I are even at seven or eight, but Jack's a member of the club so he has a lot of home field advantage.

One of the most exciting things on that first round occurred when we got to the Amen Corner. You come up over the fairway. There's a hill and you look down, and you can see it the way you've seen it on television all those years, with the Hogan Bridge at the 12th green, and the most exciting thing for me is that the first time I played Amen Corner, I played it one under. You know, I've watched guys lose the Masters on Amen Corner.

So those are some of the small details you remember, and then the experience just continues, seems to expand. For instance, you play 36 at Augusta, you get off the course, you change into your jacket, and you walk into the clubhouse to have dinner. After, you walk upstairs to have a glass of port on the balcony overlooking the 18th. If you're a true golfer who loves the game and that setting doesn't stir you, you really shouldn't be playing golf.

Have I learned anything from golf that has helped my job? When you have a bad moment on live TV, first of all, it seems bigger than it actually is. It seems like it takes twenty minutes to unfold when, literally, it goes by like that. And if you sit and worry about what just happened, then the next moment of disaster is just around the corner because you're not concentrating. So I've learned on television also to just put those bad moments quickly behind me. In golf, it's pretty much the same. I used to be somewhat of a hothead on the golf course. Never a club thrower, more of a sulker. If I hit a bad shot, had a bad hole, it affected me for the next ten holes. I eventually learned that you have to get the bad shot out of your mind quickly.

My best day in golf? Haven't had my best day in golf yet, so it could have been watching Jack Nicklaus win the Masters in '86, or seeing Ben Crenshaw win the Masters a few days after Harvey Penick died, when he sank the putt and, reaching to go get it, collapsed to his knees. If you look at golf as something more than a game, that kind of moment will stay with you.

But probably the single most memorable experience I've personally had on a golf course occurred when Jack Welch and Bob Wright took me down to a new course called the Floridian for my fortieth birthday. It's a course Wayne Huizenga built for himself. We were going to play a foursome—Wayne, Bob, Jack, and I for the weekend. But I called Greg Norman and said, "You're fifteen minutes away, why don't you come over and play with us?" When I phoned Jack to tell him Norman would be joining us, he said he didn't want to play with him, he'd be intimidated. But I said, "Jack, you're a four handicap, one of the toughest competitors, a killer businessman. This can't be that big a deal." Finally, we convinced him to play. We'd play as a fivesome, figure out a game. We decided we'd play Jack and I against Greg Norman, Bob Wright, and Wayne. We let Greg play scratch, and we put him to the tips, sent him back on every hole. And we played two best ball. So, in other words, Jack and I had to play out every hole. Anyway, it was a fantastic match, back and forth, back and forth, and it boils down to the 18th hole, with Jack and me one down. Jack misses a putt on 18 that would have tied the match. But the kicker is, Jack missed the putt for a 68. The guy who didn't want to play and thought he'd be intimidated shot a 69 against Norman, who shot 70.

It was one of those amazing days, with Welch having a career round on the afternoon that he's playing Greg Norman. I never felt better for someone else. I shot a 78. The other guys, I don't remember what they shot, and we lose one down, but it was the most rewarding loss I've ever had in my life.

During the interview Jack later had with *Fortune* or *Business Week,* the interviewer suggested that being head of GE was probably the most exciting thing that ever happened to Welch. Jack said, "No," and got his secretary to bring in the scorecard with our match against Greg Norman. "That's the most exciting thing that ever happened to me."

When I read the interview, I called Norman to tell him. Greg, being the most gracious guy in the world, immediately sends Jack a fax, saying that Jack really needs to get a hobby or something. "You need," Greg writes, "to discover something else to find thrills."

DAVID LEADBETTER

David Leadbetter, one of the world's foremost golf instructors, became well known in the 1980s for helping Nick Faldo rebuild his golf swing from scratch. Faldo went on to win six major championships. He currently works with many other top PGA and European Tour pros, including Ernie Els, Nick Price, Charles Howell III, Aaron Baddeley, and Justin Rose. Leadbetter operates twenty-seven golf academies around the world, and has also written several popular instructional books, the most recent of which is called 100% Golf.

I grew up in a small city out in Zimbabwe in Southern Africa, with the likes of Nick Price, Mark McNulty, and Denis Watson—whom, as it turned out, all played a big role in my career. Golf was the pastime kids played during their summer vacation from school. My dad got me into golf originally, and I just found the game very intriguing from the start. I got to be a fairly good junior player, but went a slightly different route from my peers—in fact, when I became an assistant professional at the club where I was a junior member, I was a three handicap. I turned professional at the young age of eighteen after attending college for only a year. Academics were just not my scene. I developed my game tremendously over the next two or three years to a point where I thought I had a chance to make the grade as a Tour player. All the while, to supplement my income, I was enjoying and learning the art of teaching the game to the club membership.

I played on the South African Tour during the summertime for about four years then went back to the United Kingdom, where I was born, and played a few tournaments on the European Tour. I was in a difficult position, though, because you couldn't get much money out of Zimbabwe in those days—there were problems with foreign exchange because of the political turmoil in the country at that time. Not to mention the money on the Tour in the mid to late 1970s was not what it is today. In short, without a sponsor it was very difficult for a young player to stay afloat financially—unless you were one of the top players.

Despite not possessing a big bank account, and having only made a little money through playing in pro-ams and doing a bit of teaching, I decided to go to the European Tour Qualifying School at a course called Foxhills just outside of London. I ultimately missed the 72-hole qualifying for the Tour by one shot—despite making a 2 on a par-4 on the back nine the last day. This sort of made up my mind right there not to pursue a career as a touring professional. I thought if I missed the Tour by that margin, maybe somebody was trying to tell me something. It's funny how things work out as it might have been a whole different story if I'd gained my card, as I had sponsors lined up, and teaching golf might not have been in the picture—at least for a while. I really feel fortunate that I chose the path that I did. Teaching the game has been a real passion of mine—one which I have never lost.

The first professional who really influenced my thinking on the game when I turned pro was Simon Hobday, someone I'd watched a lot growing up. Simon is just a great character, as well as a former U.S. Senior Open champion. I didn't give him lessons per se; we just had a lot of in-depth discussions about the swing. Simon was a great ball striker with a very simple swing. He reminded me of Ben Hogan in a lot of ways, and I was very interested in the Hogan philosophy at that stage. Studying Hogan's *Modern Fundamentals* book was a template for a lot of what I would teach—so much so that I found it worthwhile to discuss his ideas in a book I wrote years later called *The Fundamentals of Hogan*. Obviously, I watched other golfers too—Gary Player in particular. Player was the man everybody in our corner of the world idolized. He was a relatively slightly built man who was still extremely strong, and had tremendous desire and a great work ethic. So he was very influential to a lot of young players at that time.

When I think back about it, my teaching was initially based on a mix of what I had learned from reading, discussing instructional techniques with friends and colleagues, things that I had experimented with, trial and error, and a lot of enthusiasm. Hopefully I didn't ruin too many golfers!

My thinking has obviously evolved since those early years. I think that although my knowledge of the game has grown tremendously, the aspect that has really improved through the years is my ability to communicate with a wide variety of players in the simplest terms. I have been very fortunate to have through the years had the opportunity to teach some of the world's greatest players and I can honestly say that these players have been my greatest teachers.

My good friends Price, Watson, and McNulty—then later Faldo and Els—and now the young future stars like Charles Howell III, Aaron Baddeley, Justin Rose, and Ty Tryon, have all played a huge role in making me into the teacher that I am today. Even those students I messed up years ago all helped shape my career.

Back in 1981, when I was teaching at Grenelefe Resort in central Florida, a young girl just out of college named Kelly Fuiks approached me to work with her on her game. She'd already won two USGA Publinks Championships and was the top player on the Arizona State golf team. She worked with me for a while and her game really improved. She then asked me if I would caddie for her in the LPGA Qualifying School at Colorado Springs Country Club. So I said sure, why not? I thought if I could follow the basic rules of caddying—show up, keep up, and shut up—I would do fine.

The qualifying requirements on the LPGA Tour back then were you got your card if you broke 300 for four rounds on a tough course, which was the standard in those days—though not today, as the quality of play has dramatically improved. Approximately ten or twelve players would qualify at each school. Obviously, I was really hoping to help Kelly get through. Needless to say, for anybody at Tour School, it's a very nerve-wracking experience for both the player and the caddie. I vividly remember stupidly wearing a new pair shoes at the tournament, and they gave me the worst blood blisters on my heels that you've ever seen. I actually got a special dispensation from the LPGA to wear flip-flops—that's how bad it was. So as it turned out, I was having a hard enough time just getting around, much less helping Kelly get her card.

Despite the caddie, she was playing pretty well and seemed to have things under control. What they did back in those days, which was amazing to me, was on the last day place a big board between the 9th green and the 10th tee, showing each player what they needed to shoot on that back nine in order to break 300. Well, you can imagine the kind of extra pressure that was put on those players who happened to read it—which was most of them I think judging by the choking that went on.

Kelly needed a 40 on the final nine to shoot 299. I was hoping that she didn't notice the board as we walked by. Well, she did. She double-bogeyed the next two holes, and I said, "Come on, Kel, don't worry about it. You're fine. That's the last shot you're going to drop." And she snapped back, "Hey, I don't need to hear that. Keep your mouth shut and let's go." I forgot the golden rule!

So, as a diligent caddie, I didn't say a word, but thought, *Oh boy, here we go!* She righted the ship and made five pars in a row. With two holes to go, she needed to par in to get her card. I wasn't sure whether she knew how she stood or not. I'm sure she did, but I wasn't going to ask her. For all of my experience as a golfer and as a teacher, it was still an extremely odd situation for me to be in. To be walking alongside a player under tremendous pressure, knowing the outcome was completely beyond my control.

Anyway, the 17th hole was a very long par-3. She hit a three-wood to the front edge of the green, chipped to about a foot, and made the putt for par. The finishing hole was a short par-4. She hit a good three-wood from the tee, and an eight-iron to 20 feet. She then proceeded to blast her first putt four feet past the hole. The next stroke would be number 299! Everything came down to those *four feet*!

She made the putt—kind of fumbled it into the hole—and the relief was enormous. I was thrilled for her as it meant so much to her and her parents, and gave me a lot of satisfaction knowing that I had helped in some way. The rest of the story, the real happy ending, is that we ended up getting married. We've been married now for nearly twenty years and have three wonderful children. Who knows what would have happened if she hadn't holed that little putt. I sometimes wonder. The fact is, that day, the way it turned out was my best day in golf.

JACK LEMMON

Jack Lemmon appeared in more than eighty films, winning Oscars for best actor in Save the Tiger *and best supporting actor in* Mister Roberts. *The star of Neil Simon's* The Odd Couple *enjoyed golf's singular blend of group and individual competition.*

I started playing golf somewhere in my early to mid-thirties (late 1950s or early1960s), when two old friends called and said, "Do you want to play with us?" I had some clubs of my dad's sitting in the garage, and I said, "Sure." So I went with them. Gradually, it evolved into once a week, and we've been at it for a long time. One guy is named Fred Shorten, who used to own the Raleigh Studios in L.A. He went to class with me at Andover. The other is a mutual friend, Biff Elliot, who's an actor and a teacher. I first knew Biff in the early live-TV days back in New York.

My best day in golf occurred on a public course out here in California called Cainaria Springs. Playing with Biff and Fred, I was shooting even par through the first three holes. We have a mini-tournament that's known as the Farfel Cup. I call my wife, whose maiden name was Felicia Farr, Farfel for fun. So we had the Farfel Cup to shoot for, which doesn't mean a damn thing except that I once went out and bought a beautiful cup. We've had it engraved once, and that was the first year, when Biff won. But we haven't bothered to engrave it since, although we continue playing for the Farfel Cup, which lasts five rounds. Once someone wins it, we start all over again.

Anyway, I was even par through those first three holes. The fourth is a tough hole, a long par-4 downhill and uphill on the second shot, which is well over 200 yards, assuming you've hit the first shot out into the fairway. So I hit the first shot and it's a good one, but I have about 210 to 215 uphill. I don't carry a three-wood, so I took out a four-wood, telling myself, "I'll probably get close." I hit the four-wood pure, and we watched it. It bounced onto the green and it kept going, going, and when it stopped, it fell into the cup.

If that was the best shot I ever made, and it was, the craziest thing that ever happened to me on a golf course was at the AT&T, playing with Peter Jacobsen. It was a Saturday at Pebble Beach and I was in one of those condos right along the first fairway. We were on the bottom floor with a little porch. I woke up kind of late and I was having breakfast in the room with Felicia and we were talking. Suddenly, she mentioned that it was 9:15 and I had a 9:50 tee-off. So I go roaring out the porch door, right beside the first fairway, then down the pathway, where people were already lined up, because players had been teeing off for at least an hour. Peter was waiting, and there we were on the first tee. I took out my driver, hit without warming up, and of course, I struck it too hard and hit a low, fading screamer right into the crowd. I'm shouting, "Fore, fore!" People part like the Red Sea in front of Moses. The ball disappears behind them and where does it go but right through a certain glass door and into my house, where Felicia's in the bathroom. She said it sounded like a machine gun going off. She didn't know what was happening.

Let me give you an idea how important golf is to me: I won't start a film if it interferes with my being in a tournament. And talking about films, I'd love to do a golf movie. I haven't so far. But Clint Eastwood, who's a close pal, has optioned the best golf book I've ever read, *Golfing in the Kingdom*. If he ever gets around to filming it, I hope to have a part. I've been fortunate enough to have played with a lot of wonderful people. Over the years, I've played with just about everybody, recently the guy who comes to mind is Jim Garner, a marvelous golfer. He's got two very bum knees now, yet he can still hit a seven-iron about 180 yards. He's adapted so he can just turn his hips at the right moment in his swing, rather than the lower part of his body, to get power. But he hates to play the AT&T now. They'd give him a cart because he can't walk the course now. But he won't take it, because nobody else uses a cart. It's one of those things.

I only got Walter Matthau out on the course with us once. When we were finished, he was dying and told us we were keeping him away from his bookie for too long. I never got Walter back on the links.

HUEY LEWIS

Huey Lewis and the News have cemented their reputation as one of the iconic bands of the 1980s. The San Francisco–based group created the kind of exuberant, party-friendly music that spoke to working men and white-collar types alike. The result was two chart-topping albums, Sports *and* Fore!, *as well as roughly ten Top 10 singles, including "The Power of Love," "The Heart of Rock 'n' Roll," "I Want A New Drug," "Stuck With You," and "Doing It All for My Baby." The band remains a popular concert attraction, but one of Lewis's favorite pastimes on the road is trying out some of the best golf courses the nation has to offer. He plays to a five handicap at the moment, though he quickly adds that he's usually closer to a seven or eight.*

There's no such thing as a bad golf course. Some are better than others, of course, but the band and I have gotten to know some of the better ones, like Oakland Hills, near Detroit, or Brookline, or Newport Country Club outside of Providence, Myopia Hunt Club near Boston, and Garden City Men's Club on Long Island. just by touring around. Augusta National is definitely a place where you feel really fortunate to play. I was lucky enough to stay in one of the bungalows there, the Eisenhower Cabin.

Even though I have the chance to play more often on the road, playing in California still gives me the best feeling. As far as the tournament cycle goes, I pretty much only play at the AT&T Pebble Beach Pro-Am—I try to make it every year. I've played about fifteen years in a row. As a two-man best ball event, it's a unique format, and it's very competitive for the amateur because only twenty-five out of maybe 150 teams make the cut. The pro has to play well to carry the team, obviously, but there are also opportunities for the amateur to help. I enjoy that.

My favorite round of all time, at least in a competitive sense, was playing with Peter Jacobsen a couple of years ago, after he played with Jack Lemmon for all those years. We were paired with Scott McCarron and Chris O'Donnell. We played really poorly at Spyglass in the first round, and not that much better at Pebble the next day. On the third day at Poppy Hills, my son came down to caddie, which was a treat, and he was a good luck charm that year. I shot 76 that day and we wound up making the cut by a stroke after I got into a groove on the back nine. In all those years, Peter had never made the Pro-Am cut with Lem, even in the year he won the tournament itself. But Lem is never far from our thoughts—I played in his group for a couple of years. He really was the man down there, "the celeb," and the galleries just loved him. It's kind of funny that he never made the cut. His last year, Peter and he were in the hunt, and making the cut was a certainty when it got rained out, so the golf gods had it in for him. He was heartbroken.

It's too bad, because that tournament really was amazing television, with Mark O'Meara and Tiger playing in a hurricane on six, and Bill Murray out there with a silly hat almost blowing off his head. For fans, it's just great to see these guys brave the elements, because usually when you tune in, they're having an easy time in Arizona in shirtsleeves putting ten-footers for birdies. But that day there were *conditions,* and I remember O'Meara in particular was really enjoying himself. He hit a knockdown six into the wind from about 120 yards and looked at the camera and said: "Pebble Beach. This is what it's all about." Tiger was kind of smiling about it, too, but the whistle deprived of us seeing some really fun, really weird golf. The celebrities and the pros, we're having a ball with the thing because it's insane. When you're playing in a gale, it's really fun, because you never know what's going to happen next.

But to go back to that round at Poppy Hills, I remember my son, who was maybe fifteen at the time, insisted on taking the huge Titleist tour bag that the company gave me with my name splashed all over it. The course was wet, and my friend Deacon Lewis told him it's by far the hardest of them to caddie. I suggested the carry bag, but Austin told me no, we have to carry the big bag with the umbrellas and the rain gear. It's tough enough for me to walk the course! But he packed for me all day Saturday and never complained. I kept saying, as we went up the hills, "You all right?" And he'd say, "Yeah, I'm fine." When we made the cut he went out and did it again on Sunday. Austin never said a word until the end of the round when he said, "Dad, Deacon was wrong. Pebble Beach is much harder." So that was kind of funny. I was proud of him. It's not as easy as it looks.

Every once in a while someone asks me the best piece of advice I ever got about golf, and I've gotten a lot, from guys like O'Meara, Scott McCarron, and Nick Faldo. But Peter Jacobsen probably taught me the best lesson. We were playing a practice round at the AT&T, sometime in the mid-1980s, and I was really nervous and self-conscious. We were playing a long par-4, and I hit a bad drive and flubbed a fairway wood. I got really upset and threw the club down. Jake rushed over and said, "Why did you throw your club?" I said, "Because I was pissed off." Then he looked me dead in the eye and said, "Let me tell you something. You're not good enough to be pissed off." I try to remember that every day.

Peter's advice speaks to the vast part of the game that takes place in your head. When you watch a PGA tournament, you'll see the four best players that week, who have shot 10 or even 20 under par over the first three days, start to tense up down the stretch. They will even occasionally hit a mistake shot like a ten handicapper. Three out four will crumble, because unless your name is Tiger Woods, you're not in that position every week, even though you play golf two hundred days a year. The player who emerges from the pressure then usually files it away as a positive experience, so he's a little stronger the next time out, and gradually that's how the true champions develop. But that same process occurs at club scrambles all over the world—it applies to everyone.

Playing in the AT&T is definitely a lot like performing on stage. At first, you feel the pressure—it's difficult because you're afraid you're going to hit the cameraman on your backswing, or the boom mike on your follow-through. But as with performing, you get used to it and actually begin to thrive on the pressure. It often felt easier to get up for a concert with ten thousand people in the crowd than for two thousand. But having said all that, I think golf is a quiet game at heart and it is absolutely an athletic endeavor. You can pretend it isn't when you're young, but as you get older, physical conditioning has a lot to do with your success.

I have been fortunate to play golf with a lot of great people, but I most enjoy the rounds on the road with Bill Gibson and John Pierce, the drummer and bassist in our band, or at my home club in Marin County, outside of San Francisco. Ultimately, it doesn't get any better than that. Teeing off in the fog with your pals, first thing in the morning and having a quiet round where nobody else is on the golf course. I'm a California guy, so for me it's just a perfect round when the fog rolls off the Pacific, stays with you for most of the front side, and then the sun comes out and you finish the round under clear blue skies.

BRANFORD MARSALIS

Born in Louisiana, jazz saxophonist Branford Marsalis is the eldest of four musical brothers. Over the course of his career, he has developed a reputation as one of the most inventive musicians in the world, recording with an eclectic group of artists ranging from Miles Davis to Sting. His most recent album, Footsteps of Our Fathers, *an homage to jazz immortals, is the first release on his own label, Marsalis Music. He continues to work with the hip-hop and rock-inflected quintet Buckshot LeFonque. Marsalis has also proven to be a serious student of the game of golf—in just a few years he's worked his way down to a 10 handicap.*

I picked up golf back in 1995. I had made a record with this strange alternative kind of band I have called Buckshot LeFonque, and we had a modest instrumental that was getting played on the radio at the time. The guys at Sony sent me to Minneapolis to play in a golf tournament to promote the record. So I went to Minny and met these guys and said, "Look, I've never played this before in my life." They assured me that was all right, they were just glad I was there, and they'd be patient, etc. I got up on the tee with some used Tommy Armour 845s, saying to myself, "There's no way I'm gonna miss this ball." I took a huge backswing . . . *whiff* . . . and that was all it took. I was a golfer.

I try to explain to people that it's the shots I miss that keep me coming back. I guess I'm just different in that way. I mean, I miss so many shots, that's all the motivation I need. One of my golf buddies is always saying stuff like, "Man, I had a 310-yard drive today." Well, yeah, but was it in the fairway? That's Joey Calderazzo, my piano player and main foil on the golf course. When I was starting out, he gave me a hard time since I was constantly tinkering with my swing, but building a swing that's right for you takes trial and error and a lot of practice. I do the same kind of thing when I practice the saxophone. There are times when I can practice a lot, and during the times I don't get to practice I visualize a lot. Sometimes the visualization helps more than the practice. The pro at Wykagyl Country Club, Charlie Poole, has helped me out a lot as well in getting over some of those conceptual obstacles. We really went through the swing piece by piece, very slowly. The first year we worked on the takeaway, second year the turn, third year the downswing, and it gradually is starting to come together for me. Of course, now that it's coming together, I barely have time to play.

I'd say I haven't been playing long enough to talk about one great day that stands out from all the rest—per se. I just enjoy touring, performing, and playing golf all over the world. I've played some unusual courses, and those are some of my favorite stories to tell. Joey and I played in São Paulo, Brazil, one time in the mid 1990s. We asked the hotel concierge to find a course for us. We came back after he'd made a few calls and he says, "Okay, I found you a golf course. They only take cash. Only dollars."

All right, no problem. I guess even if you're a member, you pay in dollars. So we drive out of São Paulo—which is an enormous city, twenty million people—and we get to the course about forty-five minutes later. A guard with a gun at the gate let us in, and we go into the clubhouse, where I used my high-school Spanish to try to let the guy know that we were here to play golf. Of course, this was completely absurd, number one because if the guard let us through, he should have known we wanted to play golf, and number two, they speak Portuguese in Brazil, not Spanish. Anyway, I got the point across, and we

started playing. On the second tee, all of a sudden we hear: *Oo!*
Oo! Oo! Ah! Ah! Ah! There's a monkey in the fairway and a bunch
of exotic birds flying around. Of course, at that moment we
realized we were basically playing golf in the middle of the
Amazon. They just cut a golf course out of the rainforest. It just
went fairway, first cut, second cut, jungle. Hit a hook? Go get
your ball, if you dare. I'd rather take a drop than even see one
of those snakes. Anyway, we just took our sweet time, sat
down, and talked between holes, since there was no one on the
course but us.

So I enjoyed that, but Europe is my favorite place to play
golf because with the exception of the U.K., there's no such
thing as a private club in most of those countries. Golf in
Europe doesn't have the social relevance it does in the United
States. In Sweden, for instance, it's a family game—you know,
mothers and daughters, families, they go out, they pay five
dollars or some incredibly low fee and just have fun. You can
play on the same courses that the European Tour professionals
play on for not much more than forty bucks. And, unlike in
other situations in Europe, at a golf course if you speak English
you're almost a shoo-in. Since I mentioned my best days have
always centered around being chewed up by the golf course, it
makes me think of a course I played in Holland called the Kennemer, when I was over for the North Sea Jazz Festival.

When the Nazis invaded Holland, they built a hospital
bunker so they could have German soldiers treated behind the
lines and underground, since the Allies were bombing. After
the war ended, no one knew what to do with the land, and it
was prohibitively expensive to demolish an enormous subter-
ranean complex. Then some guy came along and offered to
build a golf course on top of it. So when you play the Kennemer,
you can hear your ball hit the fairway with a clunk. It bounces
normally, but you can tell there's concrete right under the sod.
But it's an extremely challenging golf course—really narrow
fairways. I like the fact that in Europe, it's not about making a
course that's pleasing enough that hack golfers will be happy.
Their whole thing is: If you don't like your score, go practice and
come back. The number one handicap hole—I'll never forget—

was only 348 yards. It was a 180-yard shot to a tiny landing area, and then whatever's left to a green the size of a bathroom. Don't miss the green. Because if you miss the green there's a huge dropoff, and you'll never find your ball. It was one of those great holes where we just kept going back to play it over and over. And it's on the water, so the wind was howling the entire time. I lost twelve balls that day, and I swear my revenge on the Kennemer if we ever get back to Holland to play.

I also tell people who love golf that once in your life you have to play golf in Japan. We had a day off in Kyoto a couple years ago, and the woman from the hotel selected a course and set it up. She also told us to expect a six- to six-and-a-half-hour round. I'm thinking, *Six and a half hours? On a weekday? Impossible.* So Joey and I get to the course, and there's no one there but us. We just shake our heads, thinking we'll be around the track in no time.

Anyway, so you have to take a caddie. The caddie is always a woman. They wear pink or green uniforms, blue checkered jackets and white pants. They also wear these really, really large white bonnets—to shield the sun, I suppose. Then they have golf carts with electronic eyes. I teed off and said, "Man, this is gonna be a breeze." Then she hits the button on the motor cart, and the thing goes: *brrrrrr.* It starts moving forward at literally one or two miles per hour. I'm thinking, "Try *seven* hours."

I turn around and the caddie is gone. She's running like the wind down to our balls to mark them. So we get down to the fairway, wait for the golf cart to show up . . . *brrrrrr* . . . and Joey says, "Oh, man, let's just quit." Anyway, the caddie doesn't speak English, but I was able to communicate what clubs we wanted. I can count to a hundred in Japanese, and that's more or less the extent of it. I can get a seven-iron, but if I'm dying of kidney failure and need a doctor, I'm dead. And Joey was just hilarious out there. Since he didn't speak Japanese he just kept asking for his seven-iron over and over. One of my favorite things about Americans is the fact that they think people in foreign countries will understand them if they only speak LOUDER and sloooower. I'm like, "Give it up, Joey. Learn to speak the language a little." I was giving him a hard time about that.

But here's the best part. There's a mandatory lunch at the end of nine holes. There is no option. The woman has a little sheet of English phrases and she tells you: "It is now time for lunch." So I reply in my broken Japanese, "We don't want lunch. We want to keep playing."

The caddie runs off and gets a guy who speaks English. He says, "It's now time for your lunch."

"Yes, I know, but . . ."

"I do not understand. The lunch is there and it's for you and . . . lunch is ready."

And this went on for a full ten minutes. It became abundantly clear we're gonna have to go eat this lunch. Finally I said to Joey, "I think that so we don't like look like the coarse Americans that we actually are, we need to go eat this lunch because they're not gonna back down on this one." At the same time, they're never gonna say, "Okay, pal, just go eat the damn lunch, all right?" They do it the Japanese way. So, finally, we sat down for an hour, and by the time we finished lunch we just wanted to take a nap. Playing golf was the last thing I wanted to do. So, in the end, it was just as the woman in the hotel said, a six-and-a-half-hour round. And if you play golf in Japan, that is what it is. All the time, not some of the time. It's no wonder so many Japanese hackers head over to Hawaii for their golf fix. Anyway, that was another one of my best days in golf. And that lunch, by the way, was pretty damn good, too.

CASEY MARTIN

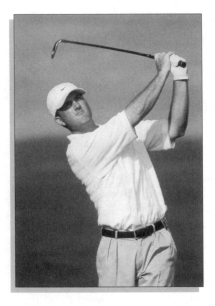

In 1998, the story of Casey Martin became headline news. A rare circulatory disorder in his leg had not stopped him from becoming a star golfer at Stanford University and a Tour-caliber player, but the condition was degenerating to the point where walking the golf course was extremely painful. He petitioned the PGA Tour for the right to use a golf cart in competitive tournaments, thus launching a controversial three-year legal battle. In 2001, the U.S. Supreme Court upheld Martin's right to use the cart, contending that this accommodation did not "fundamentally affect" competition, that is, shot-making skill. In the process, Martin's battles inspired thousands to make the most of their physical abilities. Today, Casey continues to pursue his professional career on the Nationwide Tour.

I started playing golf at a really young age—five or six years old. My dad cut down some clubs for my brother and me, and we'd just go hit balls at Eugene Country Club. I gravitated to competitive golf pretty quickly because there are a lot of good junior tournaments in Oregon. I started playing junior golf when I was about eight years old and I've played ever since. My dad and my brother Cameron were my biggest influences early on, and golf was the one sport I could play without a lot of discomfort in my leg, so I really took to it and became a strong player at an early age. I was able to play pretty much like everyone else did. My leg didn't really bother me to the point where it started becoming a major issue until I was maybe in my teenage years, but I always had a feeling I had a good future in golf if I played through it.

I've had a lot of great days in golf, but I think the most memorable for me was when we won the NCAA championship in '94, my junior year at Stanford. Playing college golf in general has given me so many great memories, but that team in particular meant a lot to me. Tiger Woods had just committed to play for Stanford the next year, so we knew we were going to be really good our senior year. But when I was a junior, it was myself and Notah Begay, Steve Burdick, Brad Lanning, and William Yanagisawa. We were ranked in the top ten, but we weren't favored to win the tournament. And the news coverage was focused all on Tiger, but we went ahead and won it without him. Thanks to Notah shooting a 62 and William shooting a 64, we got hot that week at Stonebridge Country Club, in Texas, and won the tournament a year earlier than anyone expected.

So that was the highlight of my college experience, but the next year was a pretty close second. To defend the national title and watch the best player in the world learn his stuff was pretty amazing. We got so much attention for a college golf team, it was unbelievable. We were like rock stars because of him. And it made for quite a bit of pressure, but it was good pressure, and we had a great time. I don't exactly brag about it, but I actually beat Tiger twice during those years. Both of them have big asterisks attached, but I'll take what I can get. One time in Stanford's tournament, Tiger withdrew with an arm injury, and I won the tournament, so I claim that one as a technical victory, and then another time the last day of a tournament got rained out midway through the last round, but I was leading when it was called. I got lucky. I was playing really badly, and I wouldn't have beaten him, but a lot of Tiger's opponents have realized that's the best way to go—pray for rain.

After all that's happened, I'm glad to have a moment in my professional career that matched the great experiences of my college career. In '98, when the legal battles were really at their height, I won my first tournament on what was then the Nike tour, the Nike Lakeland Classic. I remember just being petrified that week because I had all this attention and it was my first event, and yet to win it was something I'll never forget. I had a zillion people calling me, all the news networks asking for interviews and so on. Looking back, it's surprising I was able to focus and play golf.

One thing that happened around that time that has always struck me as ironic was that my manager was working on a few endorsement deals for me during that time, but nothing had been sealed yet so I could pretty much wear any company's gear out on the course. For the last round I wore a Nike hat, just a random choice I made that morning, and won the tournament wearing that logo. It turned out that my dad had met with Phil Knight, the Nike CEO, to gain his support in my legal battles. He wasn't asking for a whole lot more than that. But it worked out that he offered me an endorsement deal, and I didn't even know about all the stuff going on behind the scenes, but in the end I became a Nike athlete and I've been with them ever since. That was definitely a special time.

After that, I had the opportunity to compete in some events on the PGA Tour, which had been a goal of mine for such a long time, something I never thought I'd achieve. I'm still playing as hard as ever, and I hope to get back there soon. The game hasn't been treating me too well the last few years, so I just have to stick to it and hopefully get back to where I was. It really is a microcosm of life, as they say; it brings a lot of challenges and it can really knock you down, but it's fun when you finally get it. Golf has taught perseverance to millions, and I think it's part of the reason why my story caught the attention of so many people a few years ago. I'd tell anyone, no matter what sport they're interested in, to never let limitations hold them back. Sometimes that's easier said than done, but it's worth it to just go and have fun. More than anything, I enjoy playing golf with my family at one of my favorite courses, Pacific Dunes, for just that reason. It's just the game, pure and simple.

MARK McCORMACK

Mark H. McCormack was the founder, chairman, and CEO of IMG, the largest sports marketing company in the world. Starting with Arnold Palmer as his founding client, Mark was credited with creating sports marketing, which today is a multibillion dollar industry. His vision has transformed IMG from representing athletes into other ventures, such as modeling, music, broadcasting, publishing, and interactive media.

When I was six years old, I was hit by a car while I was crossing the street and suffered a fractured skull. The doctor told my father that I should not be allowed to play tackle football, which was my favorite sport. But my dad knew I loved sports and wanted me to do something, so he started me out playing golf. In Chicago in the thirties, it was pretty unusual for a kid to start that young, but that's how it happened for me. We belonged to the South Shore Country Club, and I played there all through my childhood. I got to be a pretty decent player, winning the Chicago Prep School championship when I was in high school and playing in a number of junior events in the Midwest. My handicap was actually scratch at one point, but I was smart enough to know that I was never going to become the next Bobby Jones or Ben Hogan.

So I continued my education and played amateur golf in college, at William and Mary, and in many tournaments after that—four U.S. Amateurs, four British Amateurs, and the national opens in Canada, South Africa, and Australia. But the accomplishment I'm most proud of was qualifying for and playing in the U.S. Open in 1958. I was actually the Medalist in my qualifying region, too. Those rounds were played at the Country Club of Cleveland, and we had about seventy-five players competing for four spots. I remember the 36th hole very well. The hole before I'd hit my drive way to the right and barely saved par, and on the final hole I knew there was an out-of-bounds area on the right, and the previous hole was still on my mind. I was trying not to panic, and I hooked my drive into a bunker. I was able to play a middle iron just short of the green and get up and down, which made me the Medalist, but I just wanted to qualify and not do anything stupid.

The U.S. Open that year was played at Southern Hills. My playing partner in the first round was Lee Mackey, Jr., who until 1980 held the lowest 18-hole score in Open history. In 1950, he shot a 64 in the opening round at Merion, but the next day fell apart and shot 81. In the round I played with him eight years later, he shot 86 and withdrew from the tournament. He was an interesting guy, nice guy from Alabama. During that first round, I remember I was one under par for the first three holes, and I checked the scoreboard later on and saw that nobody was two under after three, so I figure I actually led the U.S. Open for three holes. Eventually the course ate me up, though. The rough was so bad that players had to post a couple of caddies on both edges of the fairway as spotters, otherwise you'd lose your ball. And if you hit it in the rough, your only choice was to blast it out to the fairway with a sand wedge. I think that year the cut was one of the highest in U.S. Open history—I believe it was 157—and a lot of that was due to the cut of the rough, or lack thereof. I only missed the cut by two strokes, shooting 78–81.

I've had lots of other good memories of the game. I remember playing in Australia once with Gary Player, Arnold Palmer, and Jack Nicklaus in a practice round preparing for the Australian

Open, which was a nice experience. Also, I once set a course record in Michigan, by holing a 25-foot putt on the last hole to shoot 63, which was my lowest round ever. That was quite exciting for me. But I think my most *significant* achievement within the sport would be my establishing the world ranking system. Nobody had thought of that before, though of course they had the Order of Merit in Europe and ranking systems were used in tennis and other sports. I thought there was a real need for one as far as furthering the promotion of the sport, and with the help of Sony and the Morita brothers, who provided the computers, software, and made a substantial investment, I was able to create and execute it. Early on, it was a question of convincing everybody that this wasn't just a trick to promote IMG's clients, that it was something to really establish the best players in the world. Eventually we got everyone on board and the world ranking system became an important fixture in professional golf.

I met Arnold Palmer while I was working at a law firm in Cleveland. I had noticed that in the northeastern quadrant of the United States, where golf season basically runs from Memorial Day to Labor Day, many good clubs didn't want to turn the club over for a tournament because they would keep the members from playing for up to two weeks. But I figured that almost every member would love to have a star play the course so that when they had guests they could say things like: "Well, Arnold Palmer drove it up by this tree when he was here last week." So I convinced some of the pros—and Arnold was one of the first among them—to let me write letters to country clubs and try to set up golf exhibitions. After one of these early events, I approached Arnold and said, "Why don't you let me handle your insurance and taxes and bill-paying so you can just play golf?" And he said, "I'd love to do that. I hate that stuff."

I was in a good position to approach him with this offer since I had played golf competitively and understood the time commitment pros have to make, but I was also a lawyer and no one was really doing what I had offered to do for Palmer in those days. Shortly thereafter, Gary Player became a client when he started playing on the U.S. tour full time, and then Jack Nicklaus came up to me and asked if I'd be interested in helping him as well. So now I was representing what was being called "the Big Three of Golf." That's really how IMG got started.

Part of my vision for growing IMG was to show companies that sport and its athletes—particularly golfers—were an effective means for selling their products and services. Many of the player endorsement deals you see today, where athletes are contractually required to provide certain services such as the number of personal appearances, we were doing back in the early sixties. I remember a deal we did with the California Raisin Advisory Board. I received a letter from them inquiring about Gary Player's services. I told them I never thought about raisins and golf, so I said send me a letter about what you have in mind. I received the proposed contract, and it included ridiculous ideas. I nearly fell over in my chair. It read as follows: Clause 1: Gary should distribute raisins to the gallery during the course of tournament play. Clause 2: Gary should tell the fans, press, and fellow players how much he loves raisins. Clause 3: Gary should distribute raisins in the locker room and at the press tents. Clause 4: Gary should eat raisins as he walks from tee to green. It went on and on. After reading the whole thing I thought they wanted Gary to be a concessionaire instead of a professional golfer. But the point is we ultimately did a deal with the California Raisin Advisory Board and it worked pretty well.

I think you can tell a lot about how people conduct themselves in business by playing a round of golf with them. A round of golf brings out a range of emotions that provide insights into a person's character and personality. You know, there are some people that take pride in pretending their handicap is lower than it is and others who sandbag and try to win money from you by pretending it's higher than it is. These are two different kinds of personalities and are people you probably do not want to do business with. You have some people that will have a three-foot putt and kind of give it to themselves; in business they won't ask you for a favor they will expect it. Others who study it from both sides and try very hard to make it; and still others will go up and kind of swipe at it and if it goes in, that's fine, they've made it, and if it doesn't, the implication is that they weren't really trying, and count it as a gimme. There are all kinds of little nuances that you can watch. And listening to people describe their rounds of golf tells you a lot about them, too. There isn't a game in the world where you can learn more about a person than the game of golf.

Interview conducted December 2002.

A. J. McLEAN

A. J. McLean is one-fifth of the megagroup the Backstreet Boys. Originally from Orlando, Florida, McLean has had great success with the band—their albums Backstreet Boys and Millennium *have sold 27 million copies and counting in the U.S. alone, making them two of the top-selling albums of all time. McLean is a 12 handicap and is currently planning his first golf tattoo.*

I started playing golf when I was about eight years old. My grandfather used to be a real avid golfer, and back in the day he played in a couple of senior pro-am-type things, so he made me kind of curious about it, but I always thought it was a real goofy sport. I never thought I'd be really into it. One day, I picked up a club and broke a window at my house with a golf ball, but next thing you know, instead of getting reprimanded I got praised for having a natural golf swing. And ever since then I've been playing. I've never really had lessons, but after playing for fifteen years I've learned from trial and error.

Patience is definitely a key that I've learned from playing golf, and with my career in music that's something I draw on all the time. I think that's why so many musicians enjoy the sport so much. You can look at golf as an art form in its own right—it's very similar when it comes to how many different choices you have to make throughout the round. You can choose many different ways to approach the green in the same way that you approach a part in a song, depending on what it calls for—whether it's a really climactic point or it's a really low point, moody, soft, loud—golf has a rhythm of its own, and on TV the commentators will always use that word, *rhythm,* when someone's playing well. So it really is easy to compare golf with music.

I've started playing in the pro-ams now, and I had no idea how much fun it would be. I think when it comes to personality, Peter Jacobsen's my favorite golfer. He's such a lunatic—I love the guy to death. He's just got such great spirit about him, and he's so outspoken and outgoing. It's not like the pros really give us golf pointers out there very often, but Jacobsen was giving me plenty of tips on how to pick up girls. This was the year at the Bob Hope where myself and Justin Timberlake were the only current pop music celebrities, and it was the first time that the galleries were young. It was *NSYNC and Backstreet fans, and a lot of cute girls around. It was really weird, but Pete was eating it up.

Of course, with the fans come the paparazzi, and at Indian Wells one of them took a picture of me when I was halfway through my swing, and I just blanked. The paparazzi guy was off to the side by the ladies' tees, and he was balancing his big wide-lens camera on a metal pole in the ground. I hit that metal pole about waist-high, so basically if it hadn't been there he wouldn't have been able to have kids for the rest of his life. I came over and looked and there was a big dent on the pole. That was definitely the funniest moment I've ever had on the golf course. God knows how fast that ball was going. So that was my revenge for years of dealing with the paparazzi, my way of saying hey, back off and let me play my game. On top of that, it's pretty bizarre to have screaming girls following you around the course, too. It's not the first thing that comes to mind when you think of golf. On the greens some of the girls would be singing, "Go, A. J., go, A. J., go!" And some of them actually try to flash you, so that was kind of an aggravating distraction. When you play concerts it's to be expected, sure, but on the golf course?

My best day in golf was about three years ago, playing with Brian Littrell, one of our previous managers, and our bus driver at a public course in Washington, D.C. I remember playing a short par-4, around 300 yards, and the group ahead of us was flagging me to hit, so I went up there and drove the green. I had about a seven-footer for eagle, and of course I didn't make it, but I was so excited that I had hit the green, especially because Brian had tried to trick me into thinking that I'd actually flown over. He got to the green first, marked my ball with a tee, and pocketed it. There was a fence behind the green, with tons of balls behind it, and he points to it and shrugs and I'm like, "Oh, damn. I thought it was too good to be true." But then he let me off the hook and put the ball back, and I was just so happy. I shot 75 that day, played lights out, and I've never done it since. Probably won't again for a long time. I'm back in the 80s now.

My latest project is trying to convince my fiancée to go to Scotland on our honeymoon to play St. Andrew's. I don't want her to be a golf widow, but then again I don't want to teach her myself, because that learning would be like a third-generation tape recording, a hand-me-down, never as good as a few hours of instruction from a real pro. I'm looking forward to having her keep up with me, so that she's not just sitting in the cart bored out of her mind. Because she's been really good about letting me out on the course a lot. She knows that it's kind of my escape, and how much it's helped me with my sobriety. It's kind of my stress reliever, to be able to pick up and say: "You know what, honey? I'm a little stressed out. I'm going to go out there and hit the sticks and just feel at peace with myself." My best days in golf are the ones where I really turn my day around for the better, when I start out feeling stressed and finish in good spirits. I could talk a lot about great shots I've hit here and there, but that's really a distant second to the relaxation it gives me.

MEAT LOAF

Michael Lee Aday, known to the world by his rock alias, Meat Loaf, grew up in Dallas in a family of gospel singers. Moving to L.A. in the late sixties, he began his career opening for bands like the Who and the Stooges as well as performing in the musical Hair. *In the seventies he appeared in* Rocky Horror Picture Show, *then teamed up with Todd Rundgren and Jim Steinman to produce his magnum opus:* Bat Out of Hell—*a gargantuan teen rock opera that went on to sell more than fourteen million copies. In 1993, he recorded a successful sequel to the album,* Bat Out of Hell II. *At the end of the nineties, he again showed his knack for appearing in cult films, acting alongside Brad Pitt and Edward Norton in* Fight Club. *In 2003, Meat Loaf will release* Couldn't Have Done It Better, *his eighth studio album. Meat Loaf is an 18 handicap.*

The first time I ever played golf was in Cleveland in 1978, when some of the guys in the band went out. I didn't even really play—I hit a few shots, but I really enjoyed driving the cart. From that point on, when they went out, I'd come along and drive the cart. Naturally, nobody was going to argue with me on that. But before I started playing, I could see the appeal of the game, of just being outside on a nice day with your friends.

I chauffeured the band on the golf course for the next few years, and then in '85 I was doing a movie called *The Squeeze* with Michael Keaton. He was going out to the course on one of our days off and invited me along. So I agreed and went out with Michael and his brother and the crew's director of photography, and this time I played. Michael and his brother both shot in the high 70s, low 80s, and I was easily around 170 before I eventually quit and went back to driving the cart. The next time Michael talked me into going back out with him, he said, "You know what your problem was? You had rental clubs. You have to go out and get your own clubs." So I went to a golf store in Wilmington, North Carolina, and got some cheap clubs. I sure didn't want to spend a lot the way I hit the ball.

Some more time passed, and then I got invited to a celebrity golf tournament up at Half Moon Bay. Lee Trevino was my playing partner for the day. Before we started, he looked at my bag and goes, "What are those?"

"Golf clubs."

Trevino pulled them all out and threw them on the ground, then walked me into the pro shop and made me buy a set of Callaways. I left my old set somewhere near the first tee—never picked them up again. Then we went out and had a great round. I really like Trevino, he's just a hysterical guy. After playing with him, I felt more comfortable about playing in public events like those, because he knows how to have fun and still be dead serious about his shot making. I like playing in scrambles, because the pressure is really off. You can play someone else's ball all day, and if you make a few putts, that's just an added bonus. Making your partners laugh and enjoy themselves, that's what's important.

So now that I've moved to L.A., I often get invited out to Sherwood Country Club with a friend of mine named Brett Cullen, who is one of the first members there. I play regularly with the touring pro Steve Pate in that group. We had one round together that Steve says was the most enjoyable round of golf he had ever played in his entire life. I hit at least nine balls off the tee that hit something and went *behind* us—hit a rock, hit a tree, hit a post, hit the ball washer, and fly straight back. It was like I was cursed. On the 16th hole at Sherwood there's a boulder about 60 yards in front of the tee box. I hit that rock with maximum force and the ball rocketed back behind us at least 120 yards. Steve Pate was lying down on the tee box in tears from laughing so hard. Well, after that, I decided if Steve Pate was going to laugh at me like that, I'd join that country club and take some lessons. And I did. I've had three lessons from the pro, which has been all I've had time for, but I went from shooting 112, 114 into the 90s after those three lessons.

It seems that every time I play with other celebrities the round turns into a laugh riot. I remember playing in Cabo San Lucas at a tournament hosted by Marcus Allen and Richard Dent. I'm getting ready for my 8:30 A.M. tee time and notice there's a fifth of tequila in the cart. I went oh, no, no, no, no, no, no, no, no, no. I don't like to drink on the golf course. So I switched bags over to another cart and I'm thinking: Oh my Lord, don't pair me with these guys. I wasn't so lucky. It turns out these guys were top executives from Caesar's Palace, they were all big shots. By about the 9th hole these guys were hammered, I'm not talking about just having a little bit to drink, I mean hammered, singing as loud as they could, rolling down the hills, jumping up and down. One of the guys played really well. The more he drank, the longer his ball went, and it was always in the fairway. I played pretty well and we ended up winning the tournament. It turned out to be a lot of fun.

I think my best day in golf so far would have to be playing Cypress Point on the Monterey Peninsula with Dennis Quaid. As many golf fans know, Cypress is one of the most exclusive clubs in the world, and it's almost impossible to play that course unless you're a head of state or Arnold Palmer. Anyway, Dennis is friends with the pro at the Monterey Country Club, and the people there arranged a tee time for us—7:10 A.M. We took a little jet from L.A. and flew up there in the middle of the night for that tee time. Normally, I wouldn't get up that early to play golf, but this was Cypress Point.

When we got there, we were each assigned our own caddie. My guy had been out there forever. I made par on the 1st hole, bogey on the 2nd, par on 3 and 4. My caddie said to me, "Your swing's terrible, but you sure put the ball straight." Then he says, "Do you want me to tell you what to do?"

And I say, "Yeah."

So all of a sudden, it's like I've tapped the vein of golf wisdom, at least for this course. He says, "I've seen your swing for four holes. From this point on, I'm not going to ask you what club you want. I'm going to give you the club. I hand it to you, you hit it." .

On the greens he'd put his finger exactly on the spot for me to hit it. "It's going to break right here, turn this far, break back, and if you hit it at the right speed, it's in the hole."

I said: "What's the right speed?"

"Okay, let's do this. We'll judge speeds one to ten, one being the slowest. This one's a seven." I shot 87 that day thanks to him. I learned the value of an experienced caddie that day.

Over the next two days, my group also played Monterey Country Club, Spyglass, and Pebble Beach. By the time we got to Pebble Beach, I was a little tired. I'm not used to playing that much golf. I shot a 43 on the front nine, but it was slow going— there was a group of Japanese tourists in front of us that were taking so many pictures it was incredible. On every green, a new group picture—it backed up the course and the round took almost eight hours. I didn't play the back nine, just couldn't wait around like that and still hope to hit good shots. But it's a beautiful place, and that trip up to Monterey was one of my favorite golf experiences.

JIM NANTZ

Sports broadcaster Jim Nantz joined CBS in 1985, and has earned numerous credits over the years. He currently anchors the network's golf coverage, The NFL Today, *and calls college basketball's Final Four. Some of the events he has hosted range from the Masters to the Final Four to the Olympic Games. In 1998 he won the National Sportscaster of the Year Award. Jim is a graduate of the University of Houston, where he played on the golf team with PGA Tour pros Fred Couples and Blaine McCallister. He currently plays to an eight handicap.*

I always had this real drive and obsession as a young boy to be a network sports commentator. I wanted to cover all of the events from around the world that made such an indelible impression on me—the British Open, the Olympics, all the exotic and romantic locations that came into my living room. It thrilled me to hear the voices telling the stories of those events, how they conveyed all the drama and excitement, and I decided I wanted to be one of those voices.

I spent my youth around golf. I worked at a golf club, picking up at the driving range, cleaning clubs, and thus, I was given the chance to play all I wanted. I think golf had a lot to do with my development as a person. The game gave me a sense of maturity and responsibility far beyond my years. In golf, if you don't know how to behave, don't know the proper etiquette, and don't know how to communicate with people regardless of their age, no one will play with you.

I got hired at CBS when I was twenty-six, the youngest full-time broadcaster in the history of CBS Sports. I've often wondered, how in the world did I do that? I think the lessons I learned playing golf had a lot to do with it.

Golf was something I played seriously as a junior and I had a decent game—good enough to be invited to come down to Houston and be on the University of Houston golf team. The team at UH was extremely competitive—our coach, Dave Williams, who passed away in 1998, was a legend. He won sixteen national championships. Anyway, every year a large class of freshmen would come in and find out that they just weren't good enough to play for the team, and they would transfer out after a year. My first season, there was one freshman tournament that whole year—all the rest were varsity events. I guess you could say that one event was my best day in golf. Getting to put on the uniform, the red shirt with the half-moon-shaped HOUSTON across the back, was such an honor. That shirt is still in my closet at home, in position number one.

I had a pretty exciting tournament that day, too. I shot 35 on the front with eight pars and a birdie. By the time I'd reached the 12th tee, the word had filtered back to me that the other four guys on my team had all shot 38. And, by the way, those other four guys from Houston all became PGA Tour professionals—Fred Couples and Blaine McCallister, who are both quite well known; Ray Barr, who had about five years on tour; and John Horne, who played one year on tour and is now the head pro back in his hometown of Plainview, Texas.

On this day I was well on my way to victory with a three-shot lead! Coach Williams made his way to my group just in time to see my tee shot on the 12th hole at Clear Lake Country Club. Well, I didn't know how to handle the success. The 12th was a very short par-4, almost drivable. But I decided to hit a two-iron, and just after the coach arrived, I shanked it off the tee, which is hard to do with a long iron, but I managed to do it. I very nearly killed the guy that was playing in my group from the other school. The ball went right over the ball washer and into a ditch, which we know down in Texas as a bayou. I took a drop and made a miraculous double bogey.

The next hole was one of the all-time easiest par-5s in the world. I doubled it. I can remember the ball landing in a fairway bunker in a dog footprint, and I started to think, you know, luck's going against me now. I doubled 12, 13, and 14. The wheels had officially come off. I went from the 12th tee thinking one day I'm going to be playing in the Masters, to the 15th tee saying to myself, *Okay, let's just remember my goal was always to broadcast the Masters.* I managed somehow to right the ship and gather myself to par in. So, I shot 35, 42–77. People ask me sometimes what my stroke average was at Houston. I say 77. I always tell the story at banquets that I played in one tournament and led the entire tournament until the 12th hole the final day. Of course I fail to mention that it was a one-day 18-hole tournament. But let them conclude that I was on the 66th hole or something at the time when I erred.

It's a truism that you can really learn more about a person by the way they conduct themselves on the golf course than in any other setting. You can't really say that about other major sports. I've called the Final Four, college basketball's greatest event. How many times do I see a ball go out of bounds and both players are pointing at the guy from the other team—in many cases, they're trying to con the officials. Or you'll see coaches screaming at the refs not because they want to get the call that just went against them, but because they want the next one. *What can I get away with?* I don't expect football and basketball to be played like golf, but what it teaches kids is that you try to get away with as much as you can as long as it helps your team. In golf, you never want to get away with anything. You govern yourself. I love that about golf—at its core, the game is about honesty and integrity.

I've been very lucky and have great memories both as a player and as a witness. One of my favorite days in golf was watching Tiger Woods win the '97 Masters. I think it was the most stunning performance of the century and I don't know that we'll ever see a more important performance in the game. He had a nine-shot lead going into the final round and ended up winning by 12. That day, you know, there was a heaviness to it all. You could feel it in the air, it was palpable, that this was going to be a very vital day in the history of the game. I felt a tremendous responsibility to really be on my game, like everybody else at CBS. For a tournament that had no drama in terms of competition, every shot was framed beautifully, every word spoken was eloquent, there were no extraneous graphics, and I felt that the broadcast really fit the stature of the day.

The way Tiger won the '97 Masters at age twenty-one triggered widespread interest in the game and created all these other young phenoms who suddenly got the message that hey, it's possible that, if I worked hard, by the time I'm his age I'm going to be ready. We've certainly seen the fruits of that now. It was, one could argue, the most important day in the history of the game, and I'm very proud that I was there to document it.

CRAIG T. NELSON

Most people recognize Craig T. Nelson as the title character from the popular TV series Coach, *which ran for almost a decade on ABC. He won an Emmy for his role as the comically ill-tempered Coach Hayden Fox, but Nelson is one of those understated actors who regularly turns in fine performances in major Hollywood films.* Poltergeist, All the Right Moves, The Killing Fields, Silkwood, *and* Wag the Dog *are just a handful of titles on his résumé. Today, Nelson is the star and director of* The District, *and works on his golf game in his free time. He's a six handicap, a number he says is killing him in the pro-ams.*

My dad turned me on to golf when I was a kid, maybe six or seven years old. He had a set of Kenneth Smith's that he used to play with, and I used to go out in the backyard, and he'd have me chip into a barrel just for fun. Those were great clubs, looking back, my dad's beautiful Ken Smith irons with hickory shafts and those wonderful persimmon heads, and I was out there smashing them around. When he wasn't home, I would go out and hit rocks, if you can imagine, in the front yard. He put an end to that and took me out to the golf course. We would go to Indian River and Downriver Golf Course, the first public course in Spokane, and I always remember my father talking to me about the Spokane Country Club and how beautiful it was.

My dad was Bing Crosby's drummer, so he had great hand action as a golfer. His thing about golf and other sports, because I was mainly interested in hockey and football as a kid, was that he made me sit and watch people before I could play, and he put an emphasis on watching what they did. It got me to really look closely at body mechanics, and I noticed later on in life that he was giving me my first lesson in copying people or being a chameleon.

When I grew up, I had to quit golfing because I couldn't afford it. Early in my career, trying to establish myself as an actor, meant that I had to leave it behind for a while. I didn't take the game up again until I was forty. But I've made up for lost time. I think probably the most exciting thing that's happened to me was meeting Arnold Palmer. I met him at Spyglass during the AT&T Pebble Beach tournament. He was on the 9th tee and I was playing in the group behind him. I remember walking over and putting my hand out and saying: "Mr. Palmer, I'm Craig Nelson. I just can't tell you what a fan I am." I was tongue-tied. After all, I was meeting the King. And he said: "I know who you are. Call me Arnie." Then he gave that big smile, the one that makes everybody feel like his best friend. He's just an amazing person, bigger than life. I grew up watching him and Jack Nicklaus and Gary Player, and Arnie was the guy that would go at it tooth and nail with anything and anybody. So I'll never forget meeting him that day.

My best day in golf would probably be shooting 77 at St. Andrews on a sunny, beautiful day in Scotland. This was in 1996, and I was with my in-laws, who are really good golfers and love to play. I had an old Scottish caddie who was always drunk, so I called him Drunk Bob. Drunk Bob showed up with three pints, which he put in my bag. I had quit drinking and I'm in the land where I really want to drink, and I'm thinking: Well, hell. Then he bent my putter, and I had to bend it back into shape—all this is on the first tee. So before we had even teed off, he managed to piss me off, and I was filled with anxiety because he's got three pints of God knows what in my bag.

But he turned out to be damn funny, that Drunk Bob. Couldn't understand him at all. I'd ask him yardage, and he kept giving me meters, or he'd say: "Hit it over there. Don't go there." It was such a beautiful day and we were having so much fun that pretty soon I realized, hey, I'm not playing badly. I think I went out on the front in par. On the back nine, he's getting drunker as we go, but now I can sort of understand him! A lot of Americans believe in this mythical creature, the mystic Scottish caddie, who gives words of wisdom that change a man for a lifetime. Believe me, this was not my guy. I had a guy who was stinkin' loaded, making jokes and palling around with me. But he put me at ease, so maybe that was his secret, because everything came together that day. I wasn't in a bunker the entire round, which Drunk Bob couldn't believe. Of course, all of the bunkers have these great names dating back centuries, and he'd point them out, like, "There's the Schoolteacher's Eyebrow. Don't hit it there." Or "You'll be torched if you go into Hell Bunker." Luckily I didn't. To cap things off I birdied 18 with a crowd watching. It was just magical—I remember that day like it was yesterday.

That round was the first leg of a two-week trip to Scotland and Ireland, and I met so many great people over there. The secretary at St. Andrews really helped me out. When I got there, even though I'd made reservations in advance, had a confirmation and everything, we weren't on the schedule, but he smoothed everything over and then some. He took my reservations for the entire trip and called up each and every golf course on the list to reconfirm our tee times so that we wouldn't be inconvenienced again. To take the time to do that was really extraordinary, so I told him, "If you're ever in the States and make it out to California, please come to Sherwood Country Club and play." He did, and I got his group on the course, so I was happy to have the chance to reciprocate.

Probably my second-best memory, from a fan's standpoint, was sitting in a group at the Lexus Challenge with Ray Floyd, Gary Player, Dave Stockton, and Lee Trevino, and hearing the stories of Hogan, Sarazen, Hagen, and Bobby Jones, as well as hearing about *their* own best days in golf in their own words. Just hearing them pass on those stories, and talk about how the game has changed and what it takes to be a professional golfer was something I never thought I'd experience. Later I got to take a lesson from Dave Stockton, played a really fun round with Trevino, and I would try to emulate their swings, and it occurred to me I was doing the same thing I'd been doing ever since I was a kid.

The point is, you keep trying to improve, year after year. It makes me think of my golfing partner, Al Bello. He's a former jazz drummer in his seventies, and this guy can *play*. You don't meet many people that age who can hit the ball 280 yards. I've talked a lot about emulating swings, but Al shot 76 and beat me pretty good, but he has a swing that has never existed before in the history of golf. You wonder how he even hits the ball! But then it's easy to go back and look at so many great players—Ray Floyd, Jim Furyk, Ernie Els—who had swings that looked unusual to others, and in a way it cuts to the core of the game. The swing is a function of a personality. Look at how Palmer choked the club and attacked the ball. Some guys are just completely pure in that way, and that's what's so interesting and fun to watch. Whether it's on TV or out on the course with a guy who's about to take the match from you, it's great seeing strange swings that work well and think to yourself, *How the hell does he do that?*

CHRIS O'DONNELL

Chris O'Donnell began his career in TV commercials as a teenager, and quickly graduated to the big screen, where his good looks and natural acting approach have served him well ever since. Some of his most famous roles include playing opposite Al Pacino in Scent of a Woman, *the Caped Crusader's sidekick Robin in two* Batman *movies, and the leading role opposite Minnie Driver in* Circle of Friends. *O'Donnell plays to a six handicap.*

I'm the youngest of seven, so I grew up watching my brothers and sisters play sports and learning from them. One of my brothers is a lifelong golf nut—he played competitively in high school and a couple years at UCLA. I played every day as a kid. In the summertime, our family's summer house was on the 15th hole of a little public course called West Shore, near Lake Michigan, so we'd be out there beating balls around, and then as I got a little older, I started playing junior golf in Chicago. But I was tiny for my age, so I couldn't hit the ball with authority. A 175-yard drive was huge for me. I started working as an actor when I was about fourteen, and that kind of took me away from golf for a number of years—my time and energies were focused elsewhere.

Then when I went to college, it just turned out that all my best buddies were on the golf team, and I got into it again. When I was working on films, I'd sometimes have a lot of free time in the afternoon, and it became my pastime. By this time, I was older and stronger, and I really surprised myself. That was when I really got hooked. Today, I play as much as my marriage and fatherly duties will allow. I've got two kids now, so there's a guilt factor as well. When I'm on location, it works out pretty well and I wind up on a lot of little local tracks in random places. And sometimes I'll get to play the great courses through friends and other connections. It's amazing how small the golf world is once you start playing a lot.

A friend of mine invited me and my wife, Caroline, to Augusta for a couples' weekend. I told him I didn't think she was ready for Augusta because she usually likes to play nine holes when there's no pressure and that's about it. She agreed to go but didn't bring her clubs because she wasn't sure she was going to play a lot. After a couple of rounds my host says, "I'm a little tired. Why don't you and Caroline go out and play by yourselves." We line up a couple of caddies and they bring out this set of old blades for her to play with. They were so unforgiving I couldn't even hit them. So off we go. It was the most outrageous experience I have ever had. Here I am walking with my wife towards Amen Corner. It's a gorgeous day and nobody is on the course. I am thinking about my poor buddies who would give their left arm for this day. I played great that weekend. I broke 80 three of the four rounds. I was in my own world because it was all about golf on this great course. It was one of my two best days in golf.

The other best day was winning the Swing and Bridge, which is the big member-guest at Bel Air Country Club, with my brother. They run the tournament with first day as best ball and second day as alternate shot, and we were actually leading in both categories, gross and net. My brother played very well, and I guess I was about a ten handicap at the time. But it all came down to the last day, when the competition was both balls, everything in the cup. It was funny to see guys who aren't used to finishing holes—a lot of them make huge numbers and go nuts because in country club golf they always concede five-foot putts. I just tried to concentrate and play my game, and I think I shot right to my handicap, about 80 or 81.

Anyway, the tournament got way behind schedule, and by the time we were coming down the stretch it was pitch dark. The cocktail party had been going on for two hours already. On 18, they had spotlights on the green, and the whole bridge was full of people out watching the action. We were the last group coming up, and we didn't know where we stood because there were so many people playing and it was hard to keep track of the scores. We were literally playing in the pitch dark—I could barely see the ball at my feet on my approach shot, and I made bogey. My brother hit a miserable shot but managed to get onto the green with a nice chip shot and had an eight-footer for par. On that particular green, it was a dicey situation, because those downhill putts at Bel Air can be terrifyingly quick. He sank it, and we said to each other, "You know, it doesn't matter if we win this thing or not. That was an unbelievable putt, and just a great round." We both felt so good, and we got in the clubhouse and found out we'd won by half a stroke.

It was just the coolest feeling coming into the dinner. Everyone was already seated, and Glen Campbell was singing. When we sat down it was like that scene in *Goodfellas,* when Ray Liotta gets married and everyone comes over giving him money. There was just action with everybody—Joe Pesci and all these other people coming over all pissed off, handing us cash, and my brother and I were just laughing. It was really a great night.

The celebrity tournaments are a ton of fun as well. I used to play in a tournament called the Lexus Challenge, which doesn't exist anymore, but the format was twelve celebrities paired with twelve Champions Tour pros, and they had the best guys—Nicklaus, Palmer, Player, Weiskopf, Trevino, and Chi Chi Rodriguez. I think the great thing about seniors is that they all are cut-ups, true showmen. Trevino's got his schtick, so does Chi Chi, all of them are great guys to be around. One night Ray Floyd hosted a little party at his place in La Quinta, just for the players and their wives and whoever else we had with us. I had my brother caddying for me, and he just sat there drooling, amazed to be in the room with all these legends. Then

Chi Chi comes in, and he's got this pink and white Hawaiian shirt on with his blazer and jet-black, slicked-back hair. And I say to him, "Chi Chi, that is the best-looking shirt I've seen all night."

And he says, "Do you like my shirt? Hold on . . ."

He takes his jacket and shirt off, gives it to me right there at the party. He was wearing a little tank top underneath. He put his jacket back on and went like that the rest of the night. And there I am, wearing Chi Chi's shirt. He's a little guy, and it was so funny, I looked like the Incredible Hulk wearing the thing. It's in my closet now—what a great keepsake.

What made that tournament so much fun was the fact that the pros really took an interest in your game, and you always felt involved in the action. They'd take the time to help you line up your putts. They really wanted you to play well because our net score counted toward their winnings. One year, Arnold Palmer was my partner, and I had the quintessential Palmer experience. He was in trouble on a par-5, and as his partner I figured I'd play it safe and try for par, even though I could have gone for the green in two. So I was about to lay up and Arnold comes running over and says, "You put that iron back in your bag. Don't you start playing conservative with me. Get your three-wood out." It's so typical of the attitude he's always had— going for broke. I can't even remember what happened on that shot, but I knew right away exactly the kind of golfer he is, that all those stories about his brand of golf are true.

I look forward to beginning of each year, because all the tournament information and member-guest invites come in. I put it all in my computer, so I know the deadlines to sign up for events. My wife saw my golf schedule one day and just had a total meltdown. I never intended to play in them all, but she had me show her the ones I was definitely going to enter, and there were a lot, so I had to clip a few. I have a feeling this might become an annual ritual. Overall, she is a great sport about my golf addiction.

Anyway, there are certain tournaments that come up where I've had to fight pretty hard to make sure I was able to do them. The AT&T Pebble Beach National Pro-Am, for example—I don't like to miss that, and I've gone so far to make sure that it was in my film contracts that I'd be able to compete in it. Pebble Beach is the biggest tournament I can play in, since I'm never going to qualify for a U.S. Amateur, a mid-am or anything like that. But to play on TV, with the ropes, the marshals and the tour pros, in front of thousands of people is an unbelievable rush. If you're in the right rotation with the best players and celebrities, the course is lined four people deep from tee to green. You actually get a taste of what it must be like to have a six-footer to win the U.S. Open when you're lining up a little putt to help your team make the cut. Obviously, it's a lot of fun, but also I keep in mind the great tradition at Pebble Beach, and I'm glad to be a part of it. Getting the opportunity to peek into the world of the PGA Tour pros is fascinating.

I had an interviewer ask me one time: "Would you rather have a Masters' jacket or an Academy Award?" It's an easy question for me. I'd take the green jacket, even though some people in my business would really take that the wrong way. Don't get me wrong, I'd love to win an Academy Award, but since I know I'll never win the Masters, the dream has more power. Winning something like that would be pretty sweet.

But honestly, my favorite kind of golf is pretty humble—it's just to be with my best golf buddies and play back home in Chicago at Shoreacres when there's nobody there. Literally every time I tell my wife I'm going to play eighteen holes, I play thirty-six. Every time I say I'm definitely in for thirty-six today, I'll play fifty-four. And we get up there and the first round there's tons of action, playing six point scotch with indies all around. Then a lunch break, and on the second 18 we're still walking with the caddies. By the third 18, everyone's had a few beers and, suddenly it's an eightsome, and all the guys start showing up out of nowhere. Those are easily my favorite days, because when you're from Chicago, you're used to such crappy weather, but when you have that perfect summer day, and you're at the course with all your friends, you don't take it for granted, and it's just the best.

ARNOLD PALMER

Arnold Palmer is one of the game's true legends, and probably the most popular player in the history of the sport. His aggressive style of play and friendly nature were perfectly timed with the emergence of the television medium. In the fifties, with broadcasts of golf tournaments now capable of entering millions of homes, Palmer defied the stereotype of the aloof, patrician golf professional. His winning smile and down-to-earth ways earned him legions of fans, known to this day as "Arnie's Army." This, combined with Palmer's rivalry with Jack Nicklaus, triggered an explosion in golf's popularity, both on TV and at municipal courses nationwide. Over the course of his career, Palmer racked up ninety-two professional victories, including seven majors. Today, Palmer continues to manage his various businesses and designing courses, adding a few extra touches to one of golf's most impressive résumés.

My best day in golf is every day. It's a rare day indeed that I don't have a club in my hands, enjoying every minute of it, because everything I have I owe to golf. If I could give anything more back to the game than I already have, I would, in a heartbeat. If pressed to single out one day that I would consider my best day in golf, I would have to settle for that August Saturday at the Country Club of Detroit when I reached what I have often said was the turning point of my life.

It was 1954, and I was twenty-four years old. I was certainly confident in my ability to play golf from my success in tournaments during my four seasons at Wake Forest University, but I was still sort of looking, searching, for my place in the world. After three years in the Coast Guard during the Korean War and a brief return to Wake Forest, I had taken a job as a salesman, a manufacturer's representative, in Cleveland, but I had the upcoming U.S. Amateur marked on my calendar. I'd fallen short of that title the previous year, but I'd been working hard on my game, practicing the fundamentals my father, Deacon Palmer, had taught me back home in Latrobe, Pennsylvania.

The U.S. Amateur is an extremely demanding tournament. I played seven matches to reach the final. The crowds were the biggest I'd ever seen, but it seemed like people were beginning to notice me. That year was the first time in the event that all the fairways were roped off from tee to green. Coming into the championship match, people had said that I'd moved through the toughest bracket of the tournament, but I tried to stay focused. My opponent was a distinguished veteran, Bob Sweeny. He was forty-three and a very steady, experienced golfer. As it is today, the tournament was conducted at match play rather than stroke play, which made the experience even more intense, because you're going directly against the other guy as well as the course. We had a brilliant match, and I came out on top, 1-up. I was two over par for the thirty-six holes. Although it didn't sink in at once, amid the elation I felt in having won one of the most coveted titles in the game, the victory convinced me in short order that I could compete on the pro tour.

The next few months were a whirlwind. A few weeks after the victory, I was invited as the Amateur champion to a big tournament at Shawnee-on-the-Delaware in eastern Pennsylvania. It was hosted by the great musical director and showman Fred Waring. That weekend I met Winnie Walzer, a close friend of Fred's daughter, Dixie. I thought she had come out on the course to watch me play when I saw her on the 11th fairway. I sauntered over and asked if she wanted to tag along. After chatting over the next couple of holes I asked her to sit with me at the dinner dance later that evening. She accepted, and I went about my business with a new spring in my step. I learned years later that she actually was there to watch her "Uncle Fred," who was in the foursome directly behind me. I proposed to her before the week was out, and we became engaged. I turned pro in November and applied for Tour credentials. A month later, Winnie and I eloped and were married on December 20, at the Presbyterian Church in Falls Church, Virginia. My sister Cheech made all the arrangements for us. So I suppose you could say that my best day in golf led directly to the best day of my life. After the wedding, we departed for the West Coast and I began my professional career shortly thereafter. We never looked back.

GARY PLAYER

Gary Player's fiery playing style and competitive spirit made him one of the iconic figures of international golf. Nicknamed the Black Knight due to his penchant for black clothing, the South African has won 163 professional tournaments around the world—including nine majors—and twenty-six Champions Tour events globally over the course of his career. Today, Player's passions are breeding thoroughbred racehorses, designing golf courses, and running his charitable foundation to benefit rural education. Player lists his dream golf foursome as: Sir Winston Churchill, Mahatma Gandhi, Nelson Mandela, and Mother Teresa. Now that would be a sight to see!

In Johannesburg, South Africa, where I grew up, there are about a hundred golf courses in a sixty-mile radius, and the climate is absolutely perfect year round. It's always been a point of pride for me that South Africa has produced so many wonderful golfers.

My father worked in the mines and was an avid amateur golfer. When I was young, he asked me again and again if I'd like to play golf with him, and for a long time I wasn't interested. I said it was a sissy's game. But thank goodness he persisted, because it turned out to be one of the great joys of my life. I started when I was fourteen, and at the time I was active on the sports teams at my school, so I only played maybe once a week, but in a couple of years I brought my handicap down to zero, and that's when I decided to turn pro, at age seventeen. The people who were important to me, then and now—my father, my wife, Vivienne (whom I met when I was fourteen), and my father-in-law, who was a pro—were very inspirational to me when I was just getting started, so I was lucky in that respect. My golfing hero was definitely Ben Hogan, because he was roughly my physical size, and his work ethic impressed me so much.

My best day in golf, without question, was the day I completed the career Grand Slam, in 1965. At the time it had only been achieved by Hogan and Gene Sarazen. Had I been born in the United States, it might have come sooner for me, but in those days the travel was intense—it took forty hours to fly to America. It took me quite some time to get used to that, especially because I've always liked to be at home with my family as much as possible.

The final leg of my Grand Slam was in St. Louis at Bellerive Country Club. I didn't run away with the title by any means—I had to win an eighteen-hole playoff with Kel Nagle of Australia first. And that was after I gave up a two-stroke lead with three holes to play—I finished double bogey, par, par—which was very frustrating. Still, I was in a tremendous frame of mind and focus that week; I didn't go out to dinner with anybody, and I did a lot of praying. Not to win, but for courage, and that's a very important distinction. Also, the week before, Jack Nicklaus approached me and said: Don't go to the Tour event this week, come with me and practice at the U.S. Open site and get familiar. And I think that had a lot to do with me winning the Open too. Another major factor was physical conditioning. It's so hot in St. Louis at that time of year, and I was doing a lot of weight training, partly to make up for the fact that I was probably traveling more than any man on earth. Everybody said I was crazy, of course, but I started training with weights when I was ten, and it gave me a real advantage because golfers simply didn't exercise in those days.

So I had a lot on my mind that day. Of course, I had an idea of the historic significance, though that's really something that has taken years to fully sink in. So many wonderful players have never completed the Grand Slam, men that I certainly would have expected it from at the peaks of their careers. But Arnold Palmer never won the PGA, Trevino never won the Masters, Tom Watson never won the PGA, and so on.

After winning the tournament I gave all of my prize money back to the USGA, most of it earmarked for cancer research and charity organizations, along with a percentage dedicated to junior golf. That meant a lot to me, in terms of remembering the opportunities I had to pick up the game and succeed as a young man.

I've been lucky to have a very diverse life as a result of golf. I've had dinner with presidents, prime ministers, and movie stars, and I've gotten to meet wonderful people in the villages of Africa as well. Traveling is the best education one can obtain—you learn to be well-dressed, well-spoken, and at all times interested in the diversity of the world. I would also encourage every young person to read the Book of Proverbs, because that's a college degree in itself. One of the things it says applies to sports, business, practically every human endeavor: *Enjoy the success of others because when you have success you'd like them to enjoy yours.* That's been a vital lesson for me, and it has reinforced itself over the course of over twelve million miles of travel, meeting people, and being around the game of golf for the last fifty years.

MAURY POVICH

Maury Povich has had a long and successful career in broadcast journalism, bringing his amiable style to a wide range of news topics. Starting out as a sportscaster for WTTG-TV in Washington D.C., he is best known for hosting Fox's groundbreaking daily news magazine, A Current Affair, *as well as his most recent project,* The Maury Povich Show. *Povich is a scratch golfer, and lives in New York with his wife, Connie Chung.*

y father, Shirley, who was a sports columnist for *The Washington Post* for many years, grew up in Bar Harbor, Maine, in the early 1900s, when the town rivaled Newport as a millionaire's summer retreat. Some of these wealthy men built their own course there called Kebo Valley, which is one of the oldest courses in America, and my father, like many of the townie kids, caddied there. One very hot day summer day around 1919, he and one of his buddies were hanging around the caddie area, and decided it was too hot for them to get out on the course, so they started to run down to the local swimming hole. The caddie master tracked my father down, brought him back to the course and said, "Here, you caddie for that man."

On the second hole, the man hit the ball way out of bounds, and had given up on the search, but my father ran ahead and found it. The man was so impressed he said: "You're going to be my caddie for the rest of the summer. My carriage will pick you up." In that age, even Bar Harbor didn't have many cars, everybody had horses and buggies. My father caddied for him every day in the summertime for three years, and when he graduated high school, the man said: "I want to bring you to Washington, D.C. I own a newspaper. I'll make you a copy boy." The man's name was Edward B. McLean, and he was the owner and publisher of *The Washington Post.* When my father got there in 1922, he discovered that McLean had built a golf course at his own home, and the first man he caddied for was the president of the United States, Warren Harding.

So caddying turned out to be my father's introduction to journalism. By the time he was twenty-one, he was the sports editor of the paper. It's interesting—in a not-so-roundabout way, golf really is responsible for my whole being. As a kid, I dabbled in it a little bit at public courses. We never had a club membership, because my dad had access through his job to most of the better courses anyway. Finally, when I turned thirty, my father joined Woodmount Country Club, right outside Washington. I still wasn't making a lot of money, but he put up the $500 or so for me to join, and I was hooked. It was the only thing in my day-to-day life in which the whole world just vanished—there was just a complete escape. I never thought about anything, and all I cared about was chasing the ball around. Little by little, I brought my handicap down, and I began to have this great respect for the game and I really believed that if I broke a rule intentionally, in any way, I really believed that God would strike me between my shoulder blades. I mean, it would be instant death with a lightning bolt.

So that's how I got started. But it wasn't until my fiftieth birthday that my wife Connie, as a gift, researched the whole golf teaching profession and hired Peter Kostis to come to our home in New Jersey for a weekend. She called him the Golf God of teaching. Now, thirteen years later, the Chungster thinks of Mr. Kostis as the Golf Devil because I follow him all around the country, taking lessons and playing with him. He's become one of my best friends.

Kostis and his buddy Gary McCord beat it into me that I could be competitive with practice, and a great highlight was qualifying for the U.S. Senior Amateur in 2000, and then making it to match play. Just qualifying is difficult enough—we had eighty guys for four spots in the Middle Atlantic section. Then when I get to the tournament site, which is a great course— Charlotte Country Club, a Donald Ross course—you play thirty-six holes of medal, and I finished fourteenth out of 175 guys. I was on cloud nine. The Golf Channel interviewed me, and Tony Kornheiser from ESPN is calling me, because he's an old friend of mine and was one of my father's proteges at *The Washington Post.*

I was reveling in all of this, but the next morning was match play, and I never mentally reset the bar. I never said: "Okay, that's over. There's a lot of work to be done here." I was matched up with Jay Fitzgerald, who's the former publisher of *Golf Digest,* and he's a very good player. The next thing I know, after nine holes I'm 5 down. And I lost 4 and 3, just got my tail whipped, and I learned a very crucial lesson: you just can't rest on your laurels. It's like a new pro going on the tour and shooting 63 on Thursday and not realizing you have to play Friday, Saturday, and Sunday.

From a personal standpoint, my best day in golf was in 1984, playing in the club championship finals at Woodmount in front of my father, who had never seen me play competitively. He had never seen me progress as a golfer, and always thought my older brother, David, had a better swing, even though he hasn't played a game of golf in probably fifty years. Anyway, in that match I was never up in the thirty-six-hole match until the first playoff hole, when I won the match. And he was there. He was so excited—by that time he was eighty, and following the match in his cart, and he came over to me afterward and said, "When you were 3 down on the back nine, I was holding this golf ball so tight—I was rooting for you so hard, I think I broke my hand." That was the greatest joy I've had, showing him that the game is as dear to me as it was to him.

My love for the game extends to golf antiques—my collection is getting to be pretty world-class. I've narrowed my focus to art, clubs, and balls, and I don't collect anything after the nineteenth century. I find the history of the game completely fascinating. I have a lot of old Tom Morris clubs, which are just incredible to hold and think about how much the game has changed. Some of my favorites are my seventeenth-century irons—which were at that time used only as trouble clubs. Everything else was a long-nosed wooden club. Only if you went into ruts did you use irons. There are only about four in the world that they call spur-toe irons, which has kind of a square toe, and at the end of the square toe there's an iron spur, and I have one of them.

In the area of golf balls, I've got some interesting stuff as well. Golf was saved by a man named Paterson. In the early periods of the golf ball, they were all made of feathers, and they were very expensive. In fact, particularly in the wet climate of Scotland, you could go through three or four of these a round because they would lose their shape. As a result, only the landed gentry could play the game, and by the mid-nineteenth century golf was becoming extinct. So this fellow Paterson somehow went to Malaysia, brought back this sap called gutta-percha, put it in a bowl, folded it out, and produced a very smooth, hard ball, but it didn't cost much, and you didn't have to use more than one a round. Then they found out that the more they hit this gutta-percha ball, and as it accumulated scratches and nicks, the higher it would fly. That's where dimples came from. There are only two gutta-percha balls that I know of that have the name Paterson on them, and I have one of them. So, that's another rarity.

Golf has definitely helped me shape my career, and I enjoy finding the parallels between the two. When I'm about to go out there and tape a show, I'm on my own. I've got a lot of support, great producers and everything else, but ultimately you're on your own in this business. And I think that applies to golf as well—you are truly on your own, dealing with all the elements, both in and outside of your control, and the factors are constantly changing. You have to be in control of your emotions as well as the physical act of striking the ball. It's the same thing in television—you don't know what's going to happen out there, but your reactions have to be well-measured. I don't always know how people are going to respond to a segment, but you always try to keep people interested. If you approach the game of golf honestly—and it really is hard work as well as a lot of fun—it does eventually influence other aspects of your life in a positive way.

NICK PRICE

Nick Price is one of the brightest stars of today's PGA Tour. Since turning pro in 1977, he has racked up eighteen PGA Tour wins along with twenty-four international events. He has won three major championships—the PGA Championship twice, in '92 and '94, and the '94 British Open. The two-time PGA Player of the Year won fifteen tournaments in the nineties—second only to Tiger Woods.

As far as my life in golf is concerned, it would be best to start at the beginning. I was raised in Rhodesia, now called Zimbabwe, and my brother Tim got me started with the game. He's seven years older than I am, so when I was eight, I always wanted to hang with him and his friends. When you're that age, the fifteen- and sixteen-year-olds do a lot more fun stuff than you. He took me with his friends along to the golf course, but only on the condition that I caddie for him. After a couple of holes, though, I forgot about caddying and started hitting shots myself. I fell in love with golf instantly.

We had such a wonderful junior golf program in Rhodesia in those days. During the summer school vacation, they organized these little eighteen-hole medal tournaments on weekday mornings, all at different golf courses, and the entry fee was only a quarter. We carried our own bags and just had a blast. Some of my best friends today are kids I grew up playing junior golf with.

Jack Nicklaus was my idol growing up. He was in his heyday when I first became aware of the game in about 1972. He was just cleaning up, winning everything. We bought all of his books, studied his swing, analyzed his game as much as we could—in just the same way that little kids today study Tiger Woods. And Gary Player was kind of a distant second. We all were aware of him because he's from South Africa, and was an excellent golfer as well, but the way Jack played in those days, it was hard to idolize anyone else.

Anyway, in '74 I was invited to play in the Junior Worlds in San Diego. I was surprised, because when you grow up in a small country, you don't really have a lot of competition, so you don't know how good your game is. It was a very big event—but it was also too expensive for my family. I went to my mother and begged her constantly for two months for $150, which was a huge amount of money in Rhodesia. She finally conceded, and I went over there in August and won the tournament. It was like a dream come true for me, and I realized I might have a chance to reach the next level, even though I also understood even then that junior and pro golf are totally different things.

When I came home I had to fulfill my military service, so I did two years in the Air Force. I got out just before my twenty-first birthday, and I went back to my mom. I had no idea what I was going to do at that point, and she said, "Why don't you try professional golf. You've always loved playing, and you've saved some money from the military." And I thought, why not? I'd give it a try. So I sold my car and went to South Africa and turned pro. In those days, I was just trying to survive. You measured your success by how much money you had, not because it was your savings, but because it told you how many tournaments you could play in. If you had ten thousand dollars in the bank, that gave you ten tournaments to earn the money back. The first year I made about ten thousand dollars, and I was over the moon with that, even though with expenses almost none of it was in my pocket. The second year, 1980, was a banner year, and I made about fifty thousand dollars, at which point I was almost ready to retire! My mom said to me at that point: "Keep trying. If it doesn't work out, you can always come back home and go into business or industry, or something like that." I decided to keep at it.

When I think about my best days in golf, the tournament that comes to mind was the 1983 World Series of Golf, which really jump-started my career. When you're just starting out on the Tour and are in that early stage of your career, you really don't have any guarantees. Your future hangs in the balance of how you play. My life involved going from here to there, and the life could be quite draining at times. In 1982, as golf fans remember, I stumbled on the back nine of the British Open at Troon, and Tom Watson beat me. Losing a major championship is devastating in the short term, but in the long run it's a positive experience as far as playing golf under pressure is concerned.

I played really well the first three days at Firestone, and I had the lead with Nicklaus, Raymond Floyd, Hale Irwin, and Isao Aoki three shots behind me. I had never won a PGA Tour event before, and even though I very much wanted the prize money, I was determined to take the tournament because the World Series offers a ten-year exemption to the winner. Distancing yourself from Q-School is a great luxury.

The 15th hole defined that tournament for me. I was going along very nicely—hanging on to my lead. It's a long par-3, and I pushed my two-iron into the right-hand bunker. It was the first time I had missed a green for quite a while. This was the moment when the others questioned whether I was going to crack. I could see it in the attitude of the players, Aoki and Irwin, who had hit their tee shots on the green, and I could imagine what they were saying to themselves. The Sunday papers that day had been wondering if I would repeat Troon, as well.

I had about a 22-yard bunker shot, and I almost holed it. I left it about an inch from the hole. And that just got me going. I birdied 17 coming in and ended up winning by four shots. On the 18th green, Jack Nicklaus came up to me after I finished and shook my hand. I still have that photograph—there is absolutely nothing like meeting your idol, and having him congratulate you. But that's the kind of person Nicklaus is. And to bring the story full circle: My caddie that day was a fellow named Geoff Cannings, one of my old junior golf partners from Rhodesia. It was nice, after being friends for such a long time, that he was there to share one of the biggest moments of my career.

DAN QUAYLE

Dan Quayle began his political career as a congressman representing Indiana's Fourth District, and later served in the Senate from 1981 to 1989. He entered the national spotlight when George H. W. Bush selected him as his running mate, and Quayle, at age forty-one, became vice president of the United States from 1989 to 1993. He is currently chairman of global operations for Cerberus Capital in New York. Quayle began playing golf at a young age and today plays to a five handicap.

I have had a lot of memorable moments on the golf course. One of the funniest incidents was at the Homestead, in Hot Springs, Virginia. My partner Jack Vardaman and I clipped Sam Snead and his partner out of ten dollars. As we walked off the 18th green, Sam quickly reached into his wallet and gave me a twenty. I went to my bag to get ten dollars to give to Sam. The manager of the Homestead was walking by and saw me giving Snead the bill, and he says, "Mr. Snead, are you taking money from the vice president?"

And Sam turns to him and says, "What does it look like?"

Beating Sam Snead on his home course was wonderful.

When I was a kid, Arnold Palmer was my favorite pro. I also enjoyed Ken Venturi, Gene Littler, and Cary Middlecoff. Jack Nicklaus was a little younger—by the time he hit his prime I was in college, so it really was Palmer who we all grew up with.

I played with him once out at the Annenberg estate. A couple of times I came within a few yards of his drive. Then Palmer started swinging harder and he hit it thirty yards ahead of me. Even today, Arnold is still a tremendous competitor.

I consider myself fortunate to have many friends who are golf professionals: Ray Floyd, Hale Irwin, Fuzzy Zoeller, Brandel Chamblee, Peter Jacobsen, Andrew Magee, and others.

My hole in one at Pine Valley was unconventional because I didn't want people to know. It was on number 10. I hit it past the pin and spun it back into the cup. At the time, I was a member of Congress. I didn't want the publicity and told my partners to keep it a secret. I waited for years before telling people about my ace at Pine Valley. The folks at Pine Valley are discreet, so the secret held.

In '66, after my freshman year of college, I helped Joe Dye set the pins and tee markers for the final round of the U.S. Open at Olympic. That was the year Billy Casper came from behind to beat Arnold Palmer.

I think the values of golf are the values that serve you well in life. Integrity is a major part of the game. When you play with someone you learn about that person. And also there are times to be aggressive and times to lay back and be patient, just as in life. I like to work at golf. I enjoy going over to the driving range and pounding balls and actually working on my game before playing in a tournament. It's a pleasure, even if it's tinkering with one aspect of my game. But the camaraderie, the competition, and the challenge are the most important. I've formed so many friendships on the course that have stood the test of time, and that to me says the most about the game.

JUDY RANKIN

Judy Rankin has had a lifetime of success in the game of golf, from winning citywide closest-to-the-pin contests in her hometown of St. Louis at the age of seven, to her election to the LPGA Hall of Fame in 2000. In between, she captured twenty-six Tour victories and was the first woman, in 1976, to earn $100,000 in prize money in one season. Although back trouble ended her career in 1983, she still is close to the game, having captained victorious Solheim Cup teams and serving as long-time commentator for ABC Sports. *Rankin has also written two books,* A Natural Way to Golf Power *and* A Woman's Guide to Better Golf.

I started playing golf at the age of six. My father was my main teacher and the guiding force behind my career—he really loved the game, and was a huge Ben Hogan fan at the time. He played public course golf, and I had the opportunity to hit golf balls with him very early on. It was definitely a trial-and-error kind of early education, and I'm often reminded of where it all started when I see tiny kids at the driving range today. It's funny, though, I don't see myself, and I don't think my family has ever thought of me, as a real athlete. I just displayed a little ability to hit the ball, and it kind of went from there.

My best day in golf, I would say, came as a response to probably my worst day in golf. In the early sixties, I went to the

British Amateur. It was at Carnoustie, probably the hardest course in the country. My father had never been out of the country before, and I hadn't either. I prepared really hard for the event and just didn't play well—lost my first match. It was a devastating experience. It was May, but the weather was bone-cold and the rain actually turned to hail during the round. I didn't have the right clothes for it, and I certainly didn't have a golf game at that point that could adapt to adverse conditions. My father always thought if you could play well one way at one place, it would work anyplace, and I think that kind of changed his mind. That tournament really shook my confidence about my future in competitive golf. I almost quit the game until *Sports Illustrated* called to let me know I was their next cover girl. That was certainly inspiration to get back to work.

I returned to Britain in 1974 to play overseas again for the very first time competitively, in the Colgate European Open. By now I had some good professional experience under my belt, and was ready to put the Amateur behind me. The tournament was played at Sunningdale, just outside of London, and I was lucky enough to get the best caddie at the club—a man named Ron Mullins, who was well into his sixties, and had been there since he was thirteen years old. He called me madame, and always caddied in coat and tie. That year, I played with the small ball, per his advice, and that in itself was an interesting experience. When you play golf with one kind of ball all your life and then change to a different size, you are very aware of it—the ball reacts differently. But Mullins gave me the courage to play their kind of golf.

Ron knew the lay of the land perfectly. He could say with total confidence: "If you hit your ball here, it's gonna go over here, and then it will work its way back to the hole." And if you could land that ball where he said to land it, he was never wrong. And with a golf course like Sunningdale that's weathered by time—they only started irrigating it a few years ago, before that it was completely natural—those are not the kind of things you can know playing one or two practice rounds.

Just like my previous tournaments in England, it was a cold, wet year, and as a result Sunningdale played very long. I was still a touch nervous because I had changed drivers maybe two weeks prior to the tournament. My father had gone into the closet in my garage and took a bunch of drivers that I wasn't using and had graphite shafts put in all of them. In the seventies, graphite was new—almost no one was using them. But my father came up with a driver that had a very severe, deep face—it was a Toney Penna—and he put a 3M graphite shaft in it. The club was 44 inches long and very light, so it was kind of an unusual club. I had actually cold-topped it in practice, so I had my doubts about the experiment. But I took it to the tournament and started it hitting it so long, so perfectly, that it made all the difference to me. I won the tournament by a couple of shots, and it's one of the most memorable of my career. Now that I think of it, that was probably one of the first big wins anywhere in the world with graphite because it had just hit the market.

I'm generally not that sentimental about golf, because as a broadcaster you become accustomed to looking at the sport in a more analytical way, but I think what made the day very special for me was the experience with my caddie and the friendship we developed—he then caddied for me many times in the future. Ron Mullins gave me a deeper emotional tie to golf than I think I had before, and a new level of respect and love for the game. It came from the sense of history that the English have for the game, and I fell in love with that place. To this day, I feel the same way.

It's very interesting to me that I have the kind of job that everyone wants—sometimes I think even more than actually being a Tour pro! Everybody wants my job. And I feel kind of bad sometimes for some of the young people that come out of college with communications degrees, and they want so badly to get involved in broadcasting. They ask for my advice, and here I have no education at all in that way. I have to make them understand that my entrée was having played the sport. For those people who come up into sports broadcasting as true broadcasters it's much more competitive. Certainly without my experience in the game I would have never made the cut. It has everything to do with why I'm there now.

Still, I've had a few moments when my background in golf couldn't save me as a broadcaster. One story kind of illustrates how everything that surrounds the game—the media, corporate sponsorship, and so on—has grown to such unbelievable proportions. It was in 1989, when Curtis Strange won the U.S. Open at Brookline.

In the second round, we were coming up a par-5, I believe it was the 14th hole. And Curtis had a kind of tricky 100-yard shot to the green, and I was quite a long way away from him. I was describing the shot he was looking at, and then I noticed that a boom mike or a parab mike was picking up some conversation, audible to the TV viewers as well as Strange and his caddie. When Curtis backed off of his shot, he said: "I didn't know the shot was that hard." So it was clear that he knew exactly what I had said, and I was far enough away from to wonder how that could be. Well, it turned out that there was a long row of hospitality tents up this fairway on the right side, and one of the tents had their television turned up very loud. Curtis had heard me via the hospitality television.

I wasn't as experienced in broadcasting as I am now, and I remember it made me very nervous and embarrassed, even though it was really no fault of mine. I don't remember what I said, but I just knew from my own experience what an annoying distraction that would be for Curtis. Fortunately, we're friends, so all it amounted to was a good laugh after the fact.

I actually don't play that much golf anymore, because of time and my travel schedule. Lately I've been threatening to get into it again, but it will take a lot of work to get my game clicking again. But I still have a great time on my occasional rounds, and I have as much fun playing golf with my son as anyone. He is so in love with golf and so frustrated by the game that he usually ends up looking to me like he's going to have a small coronary. As a child he was an excellent player, but as he got older he became involved in other sports and his golf game kind of went south. But he's still my favorite person to play with, because I can still see the little kid hitting all those nice shots. When he and I can go play nine holes, it's just a very good day. And I guess if I were to choose a favorite place to go, I'd pick Sunningdale or the little nine-hole course in Forest Park, St. Louis, where my father taught me to play. It's called Triple A, and I haven't been back there in years, so I often think it would be nice to play there one more time.

KENNY ROGERS

Country singer and actor Kenny Rogers has sold more than 100 million records, performed on every continent, and has been awarded twenty platinum albums and four Grammys. Best known for his song and movie The Gambler, *Kenny would give it all up to fulfill his dream of being a PGA Tour pro.*

Lots of country singers play golf and lots of them are real good players. I'm not as good a golfer as Vince Gill, for example, but the thing is I'm kind of an obsessive-compulsive. Once I get in on something I get obsessed. I have this place in Athens, Georgia, right near the university. I have 1,200 acres, and one day I went out there and built a green and sand trap so that I could work on my short game. Then I put in a tee box, and then another tee box and another green, and now I have 18 holes. I now have a 62-acre golf course in Athens.

You know it's funny, I am not sure what was my best day in golf, but I do know every golfer has great stories, and I remember one particularly. Many years ago, I was working in Alaska and I was playing golf every day. No matter where I was I sought out a golf course. Golf was (and still is) a really important part of my life.

I was in Anchorage, and at the time there were no golf courses there. I was told that the only really good golf course was at the military base and you had to take a small airplane to get there. So we chartered a plane and flew over to the island where the golf course was. The plane dropped us off and we walked over to the clubhouse and watched the plane leave. It would come back later in the day to pick us up. We went to the starter to get our tee time and found out that it was ladies' day at the golf course. No matter how much we argued, they would not let us play. We had to wait four to five hours for the plane to come back. I mean it was a hilarious situation. We were laughing very hard, but it was ladies' day, and so we did the second-best thing. We watched the ladies play and for some reason it stays in my mind as one of my most memorable days in golf.

I'm a nine-handicap golfer. I've never been better than that. I think I'm athletic, but I am not an athlete. I think an athlete gets devoted to something and he gets to find the time to get really good at it. I've always been really good at a lot of things but never great at anything. But I was happy to be a nine-handicap golfer.

If you play golf and bet on it, like I do, you can lose a lot of money. So I lost a lot of money. One day I went out and I shot two under par and it was the most exhilarating experiences I ever had because I played way over my head. If you are a golfer playing consistently then you have all three parts of the game come together. You have to drive well and you have to chip and putt well. Putting all of them together in any given day is why golf is so hard. I've always been able to hit the ball a long way. I've always been able to have a good short game. But seldom have I ever put it all together. This one day I did. I was with some people who didn't think I could beat them. I did beat them and beat the hell out of them. Nobody from that group will ever play with me again. I do talk to them from time to time, but not about golf. I really do consider that day my best day in golf, and it was not because of the bunch of money I won.

When you are a country music performer and you're on the road, you need some sense of grounding. You can't just play and make music all day long just because it gives you a sense of accomplishment. Golf is one of the most humbling things you'll ever do in your life and I think that if you can play, if you choose to play as if it is really important, you will find yourself surrounded with really good people. My son is a dynamite basketball player. I keep telling him that it is very important that he play golf because only very few people play basketball once you reach a certain age. If all your friends are basketball players you will find that you don't have a lot in common with everyone else. But most everyone else plays golf. I think it is one of those wonderful social events. Because of golf I've met a lot of people I might otherwise not have met.

Golf teaches you honesty. The game of golf is only fun if you play correctly. I think when you play by the rules there are times when it is so tempting to take this stroke, to not take that stroke, or not to do this or that. That's really what the game is all about. It is a sense of values that you teach yourself and you are only playing against yourself.

Playing golf, as I said, is really wonderful. I play a lot with my brother-in-law—Vince Kenny. I also played with some of the best in the world, and you know, that didn't help my game one bit, but I liked playing with them. I used to have an event at my house where I invited four pro golfers, four pro tennis players, and four celebrities. I called it the Kenny Rogers Classic Weekend. It was one of the most fun events I've ever had in my life. We did it for five years. We had Michael Jordan, Larry Bird, Isiah Thomas, Dominique Wilkins, and Charles Barkley, too. All those play great basketball, as we know. We also had Ray Floyd, Payne Stewart, and Mark Calcavecchia, and that group of guys play great golf. It just didn't get any better than that.

JUSTIN TIMBERLAKE

As a member of the chart-topping group *NSYNC, Tennessee native Justin Timberlake became the most popular teen idol of the nineties. The tidal wave of media gossip surrounding his relationship with Britney Spears was only surpassed by the millions of records *NSYNC sold worldwide. Timberlake's first solo record, Justified, was released on Jive Records in 2002, with the single "Like I Love You" reaching number 11 on the Billboard Top 100. Timberlake took up golf fairly recently but has already reached the level of a 12 handicap.

I've only been playing golf for a couple of years, but my dad has played religiously for almost ten years now, so he'd talk to me about the game now and then before I started playing. I'd tried golf when I was younger, but I didn't really have a lot of patience. I couldn't really keep up when I was twelve years old, I was more interested in music at that time. I tried the game again during one of our summer tours, we had a day off and Chris and I just went out and played for fun. During the round I hit one good shot from the tee box and thought to myself, "Uh-oh, I just got stung by the bug." You know the feeling as soon as it happens. When you hit that perfect shot, the ball explodes off the club like it does for the PGA Tour pros and flies long and straight just like you dream about.

Thinking about that shot is what got me back out there again. I bought some new clubs and really started getting into learning about the game. I decided the first thing I would do was get custom-fitted clubs. I figured I should learn the right way rather than with clubs that weren't right for my body. So I learned a lot about my equipment first. I really like my driver. It's an Orlimar 340cc with a Proforce 75 shaft on it, but I'm still working on consistently hitting the ball well with my driver.

I'm constantly working on my game. I love going to the driving range and just working on my fundamentals. My dad's a really good golfer, so he's taught me a lot about the fundamentals and I read a lot of golf magazines, like *Golf Digest* and stuff like that. I like reading about the pros and how they play, and figuring out how I can adapt what I learn to my game. Everyone's body is different, so mechanics work a little bit differently from person to person. Bernhard Langer's swing is totally different from Tiger's—but if you're built more like Langer, his swing is well worth studying. Watching their technique and trying to mimic it just makes your game better.

My favorite clubs are my wedges. I feel comfortable with short-game play. I leave the three-iron out of the bag in favor of the lob and approach wedges. They get me out of trouble, and I'm pretty deadly from 150 yards in. If I'm 130 from the flag and I hit my pitching wedge or my nine-iron and I'm a little off the green, I'm pretty confident in my chipping game with my lob wedge that I can put the ball pretty close and get up and down. Actually, I built a chipping and putting green at my house in Orlando so I can practice those shots. My house is on a lake too, so you sometimes I can't resist hitting balls into the water for fun.

The next step for me is definitely to take some lessons and figure out how to make the next leap. I've gotten down to a twelve handicap without any lessons, but I think they're necessary to move into single digits. The best round I've ever had was four over par in Los Angeles, just playing a casual round with some friends, and I'd like to start doing that consistently. Ty Tryon lives two doors down from me in Orlando, and he's one of David Leadbetter's students. He invited me to come with him to a lesson to see if I like the kind of drills they work on, the way Leadbetter's lessons are set up and so on. So I want to take him up on that offer. Ty's a cool kid, and it's interesting to see somebody who's several years younger than you play such a great game. I think he's the next Tiger, man. To be that good and that young, there's no telling how far his game will take him.

Golf is my favorite thing to do when I'm not working. It's peaceful and it's a release. I just like being outdoors, smelling the grass and, you know, smacking the ball. It's definitely taught me a lot about patience and concentration. I think golf has actually made me a little more of a patient person, you know, just with people. I've become a little more laid-back. It comes gradually, learning how to handle different situations from casual rounds as well as the big televised events. Watching the pros close up definitely helps your game, and they really encourage you along the way.

As for my best day in golf, I don't think I have had it yet because I have only been playing for a couple of years. However I do have a lot of great memories. It was very exciting to play in Bob Hope's tournament. I had never played in front of a big crowd so it was pretty exhilarating. We played four different courses in Palm Springs, and my partners were Samuel L. Jackson and Joe Pesci, and each day we were paired with a PGA Tour professional. The most fun day of the tournament was playing with Arnold Palmer—that was pretty awesome. Arnold is the King and attracted pretty large crowds. The gallery was different from past years, there were a lot of young girls because A. J. McLean of the Backstreet Boys and I were playing. I think Arnold enjoyed that, because he spent a lot of time talking to them as we walked down the fairway. He told me that if I kept at it, I would be a really good golfer, and that meant a lot to me. He's really cool.

Being a member of *NSYNC and touring around the country, I have been fortunate to play a lot of really great courses. I play a lot at Sherwood Country Club in L.A.. I've played Olympic, L.A. North, Oakmont, Congressional, and a bunch of courses in Los Cabos, Mexico, which was pretty cool. I also enjoy the public courses. My favorite course to play is just outside my hometown of Memphis, called Spring Creek. It's a Nicklaus course and I think it's the best new course in the world. My goal is to play all the courses in *Golf Digest*'s Top 100. I am planning my solo tour and am going to try to play in as many cities with cool golf courses as possible. This is one of the perks of going on tour. Traveling from city to city can get tiring, but golf gives me something extra to look forward to.

As fun as it is to play in pro-ams and at great golf courses, my best memories of golf are the rounds I've played with my dad. You know, we just really have a good time together. I had one occasion in Destin where I almost got a hole in one. It was a par-3, about 170 yards, and I hit my six-iron about three inches from the stick. I was, like, oh, man, you can't complain about that, but then again, to have that ace would have been extra special. Sometimes my mom plays too, and we make it a family event. When go on vacation to Destin, we'll get up in the morning and either play really early, then lie on the beach for the rest of the day, or we'll do the reverse, go play golf around three o'clock and play into the sunset. It's pretty nice either way. Those are pretty much my best memories.

PETER UEBERROTH

Two well-known items on Peter Ueberroth's sterling executive résumé include serving as president and CEO of the 1984 Los Angeles Olympic Organizing Committee, and serving as commissioner of Major League Baseball from 1984 to 1989. Today, Ueberroth continues to bring his leadership skills to a number of different enterprises. He is owner and co-chairman of the Pebble Beach Company and also sits on the board of the Coca Cola Company and Hilton Hotels Corporation. He learned the game of golf as a caddie on the courses of northern California and Chicago.

My best day in golf was having the opportunity to play in the AT&T Pebble Beach National Pro-Am in 2000. I look forward to it every year. It's one of the premier events in all of golf. It is the only sporting event where you really get a chance to be on the field with the pros during a competitive event. I was never able to shag a fly ball in a Major League Baseball game, even though I was commissioner; I was never able to compete in the Olympic Games in '84, even though I ran them. Back in 1956, I competed in the Olympic Trials in water polo, but didn't make the team. But at the AT&T, because of its unusual format, you get a chance to share the playing field with the best in the world.

One-hundred eighty pros and 180 amateurs enter the tournament. Sixty pros make the cut, and twenty amateurs make the cut with their pro. Over the years, I've played with a number of different pros, and I usually don't make the cut, but that year I made the cut with Jim Furyk as my partner. That Saturday night I was celebrating with a group of people at a wonderful Italian restaurant, Peppoli's in Spanish Bay, and somebody brought me a note that said: "Your playing partners for the final round are Jerry Chang and Eldrick 'Tiger' Woods." After reading that, I quit drinking red wine. I usually sleep like a baby, but I tossed and turned all night. The next morning, I was as nervous as I could possibly be. I went over to the course and was sitting on a bench getting ready to tee off. I looked down the bench and there's three "twentysomethings"—Furyk; Chang, who was captain of the Stanford golf team; and Tiger Woods. The three of them and a "sixtysomething." I said to myself: What's wrong with this picture?

I literally can't remember teeing up the first ball with that crowd, but luckily I hit it, and eventually made the ugliest par that has ever been made on the first hole, but it settled me down. I needed to be enjoying myself, playing with three very good players, as a 12 handicap was daunting. I don't remember much about my round, but I remember Tiger's as if it were yesterday.

Tiger had his first potentially bad hole on the 9th, but he sunk a miraculous long downhill putt for par, and from that point on he was on the warpath. He had started the day *nine strokes off the pace*. Then he posted his nine-hole score, and all the guys behind us that would come to the scoreboard at 10 would see the number and see that Tiger was starting to close in on the field. The four of us really were just having a good time, but I noticed on several occasions the television never showed Tiger laughing and having fun walking down the fairway. When he's about to hit a shot or select a club, he's obviously concentrating, probably like very few athletes can, but he's having fun out there, which is sometimes lost in the coverage.

Another thing that impressed me was how closely he watches his partners play, even a mid-handicapper like me. In an event of that magnitude, if you can't score, you get out of the pro's way, and I picked up on one hole and Tiger kind of questioned it. He said: "You still could have hit that in the hole." Later I realized why he was so interested—he's simply a great analyzer of course information. When we moved out to the 14th, we both wound up in the front greenside trap. It's a long par-5, and I was there in three, he in two. Again I went to pick up my ball, and he says: "No, no, you've got to hit it."

I replied, "I don't want to hit sand onto your ball, since I'm away."

He replies, "Just play the ball. I want to watch the sand, and see what happens on the green."

Anyway, I was lucky to par the hole, and Tiger made birdie. None of us are looking at the scoreboard on 15 (par 4), but then later he makes eagle, and the traffic on 17 Mile Drive along the course came to a stop. People start getting out of their cars—they're witnessing a great comeback and, literally, the ground starts to shake. And then, of course, he almost eagles the 16th—hits his second shot to about six feet, and birdies it. He finished with two more birdies to make a comeback that probably in the annals of golf has not been equaled and probably will never be, to be 9 strokes back and come back and win. What's more remarkable is that he was 7 strokes down with 7 to play.

Only a truly great golfer has the patience to encourage his playing partners to make the most of their shots, because he knows it will also help him, and Tiger did that throughout the round. On 18, when he knew the huge crowd would be totally focused on his putt, knowing that it will determine whether he wins or loses the tournament, he spent just as much time helping Jerry Chang line up his putt. By then he had passed so many golfers, and we knew unless there was a miracle he would win. Then he studied his putt, almost casually, just enough to make up his mind, and nailed it with the huge scoreboard behind him. I was honored to be there that day, and not witnessing it from the bleachers but on the field of play with him and everyone else involved in the tournament.

KARRIE WEBB

Since her arrival on tour in late 1995, Karrie Webb has taken the LPGA by storm. Through 2002 she has won twenty-eight events and six major championship titles, becoming the second youngest woman ever to complete the career Grand Slam. She has won seven LPGA awards, including Rookie of the Year, Player of the Year, and the Vare Trophy. In just seven years, Webb has already qualified for the LPGA Hall of Fame. She will be inducted in 2005, as soon as she has completed her first decade on tour.

My mom and dad and grandparents all took up the game just before I was born, and it was sort of just a family sport. Some of my earliest memories are of running amok and having a good time with the other children at the golf club after our parents had finished playing golf. I grew up in a small town—Ayr, Australia—and played at the only golf club in town, Ayr Golf Club. It was always a nice atmosphere there, so I guess I wanted to play golf to be like mom and dad. I started competing in junior tournaments when I was eight, and got down to scratch at about age sixteen. A lot happened for me that year: I made my first amateur side playing for the state of Queensland, and then traveled overseas for the first time representing Australia's junior team.

When I first started playing, I didn't emulate or admire many professional golfers. Mostly I looked up to my coach, Kelvin

Haller, who was one of the best amateurs at the club. As I got a little older, Greg Norman became someone that I looked up to. The next year, when I was seventeen, I won his first inaugural junior golf tournament in Queensland, where he had set up a junior golf foundation. The boys' winner and girls' winner got to fly to the United States and spend a week at his house in Florida. I have just wonderful memories of that experience. We played some golf, sure, but it really was just a nice holiday. He made us feel quite at home. As a teenager it was like the chance of a lifetime, not knowing what kind of future I might or might not have in golf. I was pretty shy about asking too many questions, but the biggest lesson I learned was that as big a star as Greg Norman is, he is just a normal person with a wife and kids. It impressed me to see someone who'd had that much success but was still interested in meeting people and helping kids just starting their careers. That visit had a big impact on how I came to view being a successful golfer.

I decided to turn pro because I had won a lot of amateur championships and felt there was nothing left to accomplish in Australia. I wanted to take on the best in the world. After turning pro, my first two events were in Australia, and then I went and qualified for the European Tour. In 1995, I won the Women's British Open as a rookie, and that boosted my confidence to know I could compete at the highest level. That convinced me to go through the LPGA's qualifying school. I came in second at Q-school, which was quite an accomplishment since I played with a broken bone in my wrist. I was in a lot of pain, but had to persevere because I knew I would not have another shot at the Tour until the following year. I didn't want to wait that long. When I came on the Tour for the first time, I'd obviously heard of people like Nancy Lopez, Beth Daniel and Betsy King, and knew that they were great players, but growing up in Australia there wasn't much media exposure to the LPGA, so I wasn't sure what I was getting into. You hear stories about how everyone's mean to the rookies when they come out on the Tour, but they really are just lies. All I got was people introducing themselves, everyone from the Hall of Famers all the way down to the other rookies, and I couldn't have felt more welcome.

So far, in my career the days that really meant a lot to me were the first two events I competed in, where I finished second, then first, at the LPGA Tournament of Champions and the Healthsouth Inaugural, It pretty much set up my life for the years to come, as I never expected I'd get a three-year exemption so quickly. After that, I didn't have pressure to keep my card, so it allowed me to play relaxed, which has been a great help ever since.

The Tournament of Champions was really special because I qualified without being a member of the LPGA. Winning the Women's British Open the previous year gave me an exemption in this elite tournament of winners. I just remember the Monday of that tournament so vividly—it was a really cold, windy day. This was at Grand Cypress in Orlando, and I've never seen Florida as cold as it was that day. Almost no one was practicing on the range. But I thought, *I have to be prepared to compete, so I'd better hit a few balls.* When I went down, there was only one person on the range, and it was Nancy Lopez, who was hitting down the far right-hand end of the range. There was no way I was going to go down and hit next to her— I barely even felt that I deserved to be on the same range.

The next week is the Healthsouth in Orlando, which I won in a four-hole sudden-death playoff with Martha Nause and Jane Geddes. Even though it was my first LPGA victory, the tournament passed by in a blur. I had so much adrenaline throughout the event that my memory of the whole thing is clouded. I remember we played the 18th hole four times in the playoffs, and I played it identically every time. I think about it from time to time as a mental aid—that hole had a tight driving area, and four straight times that day I just ripped it straight down the middle. I think when you're twenty-one you're just fearless, and I certainly didn't have anything to lose, since no one knew who I was or expected me to win the playoff. Now that I've experienced a lot of what the LPGA Tour has to offer, it surprises me that I had the composure to do anything like that.

Some of my best days in golf have also come through my involvement in hosting a golf event under my name, to benefit my charity CRPF, Christopher Reeve Paralysis Foundation. It's something that is close to my heart because my coach has been a quadriplegic for the last twelve years now. It had always been something that I thought if I got the chance, I would try to help raise awareness however I could. When I started donating money to Reeve's organization, they contacted me wanting to find out why I was doing it and if I wanted to become more involved. And shortly after that, Christopher said, "We should have a celebrity pro-am," and it just took off from there.

The pro-am has been a pleasure to be a part of. We've been working on getting a good group of celebrities to come and play, and it's going very well. One person who is always fun for the pro-am is Chevy Chase. It's funny how the fact that because he was the star of the biggest golf movie ever made, a lot of people think he's an avid golfer, but he's actually not at all. He actually prefers tennis. Of course, people then said, "Well, you could swing the club pretty well in the movie." And he replied, "That wasn't me. That was a stunt double." So, that's Hollywood magic for you, because to this day everyone thinks he can play.

I think golf can be a really powerful tool in a lot of different ways. I've mentioned Christopher's and my work through the game, but another way is its ability to teach kids the value of being courteous and sportsmanlike. I think out of any sport, golf has a unique ability to teach those values, along with patience and discipline. If you want to be good at golf, you do have to be disciplined—it's just like anything in life in that respect. But for most people, it's more important to play the game with good sportsmanship, regardless of whether or not you're a strong player. That's the best way to get the most enjoyment from the game.

The game has given me so much enjoyment in my life and I have been fortunate to have achieved so much so quickly. I have achieved more than I ever dreamed possible. At the beginning of each year I always set goals for the season, now I'm actually having trouble setting goals, so I set dream goals. As far as a dream achievement, I don't have a specific idea of what it is. I will continue to compete because there is a lot to achieve.

JACK WELCH

Trained as a chemical engineer, Jack Welch was the CEO of General Electric from 1981 to 2001. During his two decades in the top position, his managerial skill and business acumen became legendary, as he led the blue-chip GE to new heights of profitability and popularity. This became evident when his book Straight from the Gut *was a number-one best-seller on several lists. Today, the semiretired Welch gets to play golf regularly, though he admits his best days in the game are behind him. Still, he plays to an eight handicap.*

I picked up the game of golf when I was a kid, caddying at Kenwood Country Club in Salem, Massachusetts. I saw it mainly as a way to make some money. My favorite sport when I was a kid was hockey—it was my passion—and I came to like golf because of its similarity to hockey. But my initial interest was making a few bucks and playing on Caddie Day. I learned a lot about life from that experience. You learn a lot about behavior, you learn those who tip and don't tip, those who treat caddies well those who don't. It was quite an experience. I have a great respect for caddies—most of the time they love the game as much as you do. I think it's a funny thing when a person asks a caddie whether to shoot a six- or seven-iron, and the guy's barely seen you play, but most of the time he still picks the right club, and he'll tell you if he doesn't know. But when the guy hits a bad shot, who does he blame?

My best day in golf is pretty easy for me to pick out. I play quite a bit out on Nantucket with a friend by the name of Jacques Wullschleger, who is a very good golfer. He's the best at Sankaty Country Club—a scratch golfer. He retired early, plays almost every day year round, and plays at all kinds of senior tournaments. He is much better than I, and gave me two shots a side in the early nineties and four today.

In 1994, the last week in August, we played in the club championship against each other. I had won the club championship in '92, after Jacques got knocked off in a fluke. So he was looking to beat me this time. In the Club Championship, we played straight up. I didn't get my normal two shots. Our match went 37 holes.

It was a beautiful, breezy day out on Nantucket, and we were playing in front of a good little club crowd, twenty to forty people following us on the course. In the morning round, he shot 76 and I shot 74. In match play, we were even after nine, and I birdied 18 to go 1 up by chipping in. And then in the afternoon round, I picked up three birdies on par-3s, and I went from 1 up after 18, to 5 up after 7. And then I started to fade. He birdied 8, 9, and 11, and then I was 3 up with 4 to play. He won the next three holes; we're even and I'm leaking oil. I had to sink about a six-foot putt on 18 to stay alive and force a playoff, which I sank. That was really gut-wrenching. Finally, on the 37th hole, I made a 15-footer to beat him. I had seven birdies on the day. Now, Jacques could beat me 99 days out of 100, so it was an incredible feeling.

The funny thing was that I really owed it all to Jacques himself. During the tournament, I had some swing problems during the early rounds, and I came down to see him on a Friday night. He gave me lessons to fix my swing—and with his help I won the Saturday match and then the final!

So that's a day I'll never forget. We played straight up, a scratch handicap versus a five. That day I played right out of my mind, and that's one of those life experiences that are just special. We went to dinner that night because we said the winner had to buy dinner.

Golf is one of my favorite pastimes because of the friendly rivalries I've developed on the course. As I mentioned, I have that rivalry with Jacques Wullschleger, but I also have one with Scott McNealy of Sun Microsystems. We had been ranked one and two as far as CEO golfers go. One day, Scott sent me a fax that said, "You're number two, and I'm number one. But I don't want to be number one on a chart, I want to be number one because I beat you, and I'll play you anywhere."

Well, I took the challenge and replied: "If you'll come to Nantucket, we'll play 36 holes." So he came, and Jacques Wullschleger came out and played with us, but also served as our witness. We played 18 at Sankaty and 18 at Nantucket, and I beat him. We were pretty close at Nantucket, but I killed him at Sankaty, something like 5 and 4. We played Augusta the following year and I beat him 2 and 1 over 36 holes. A couple of years ago he did beat me, but I keep teasing him by telling him it was only an 18-hole match. Now, I've never played him on his home turf, and I know he's a considerably better golfer than I am, so in the long run he'd bury me, My strategy is to try to pick my battles wisely, especially since we play scratch and the bragging rights are pretty significant. We're both competitive guys so while it's really great fun, the outcome does matter.

BOB WRIGHT

Bob Wright, chairman and CEO of NBC, has achieved the longest tenure of any network TV executive in history. His golf game has suffered as a result. He is an avid golfer, who is frequently paired with Jack Welch, former CEO of parent company General Electric.

My handicap is an 18; it's never been lower than a 15. If I played today, I would be a 25, because I haven't played in two or three months. That's one of the sacrifices of my job— I'm a prisoner. You may think I'm in the television business, but I'm really in the delicatessen business. We have meetings and serve sandwiches all morning, take a break, and then we have meetings and serve sandwiches all afternoon and evening.

So many people use golf for business, and I think I know why. It's very hard not to know somebody fairly well after 18 holes. You get to learn a lot about them. It's very difficult to assume a false personality for 18 holes of golf. If somebody wants to appear to be a different type of person than he or she is, it usually will break down over 18 holes. I always find that to be kind of a fascinating thing. It's not like a business dinner. When you're at dinner, you're static, you have a chance to think about what you're going to say and you can manipulate a conversation. You can't do that when you're playing golf, because the physical aspects and the pressure distract you.

The pressure in the game of golf is one of its most interesting aspects. Men and women who are CEOs, doctors, and surgeons, particularly, play golf for relaxation, yet the words *pressure* and *concentration* always come up. My wife doesn't understand why I play golf, because of the pressure I put on myself, along with the hostility and anger. But I tell her it's almost like playacting, and it's a great relief. Because when I'm playing golf, I'm not good enough to be able to think seriously about anything else, so I can't carry my work around out there. If somebody is a doctor, they can't take that to the golf course, because it just doesn't work. I think that's one of the things that oftentimes women don't see about men. Hunting is the same thing. You do these things that become preoccupying and they become satisfying just because you aren't carrying around your normal worries.

As far as my best day in golf, there are a few memories that come back. Three years ago, I was over in England with Johnny Carson and our wives. We take a trip together every year and that year we went to Gleneagles, an old resort in Scotland outside of Edinburgh. Johnny was and is a good athlete. During a relatively short period when he was living in New York, he took up golf, played pretty well, and joined the Westchester County Club. He had a 12 handicap, which is quite remarkable for somebody that never played before, and then he never played again. He took up boating and he did that for a while. Then he took up tennis, and he's played that for a long time. But this was a while later, when we were at Gleneagles and he just didn't have any interest in playing golf any more. So I didn't have any clubs or anything, but as a gift, my wife got me a tee time at St. Andrews. So I drove over there and I got a European professional who was a touring pro from England, not anybody on a leader board level, just a teaching and touring pro, he met me there and we played, just the two of us.

I had never played St. Andrews. I'm not a great golfer, but that day, for nine holes, I was spectacular. I was just doing what the caddie told me to do. Everything I did was great, shots off the tee, putting, chipping, everything. I was on the 9th tee and all I had to do was get a par to give me a 39 for the front nine. I ended up with a bogie, so I got a 40 in the front nine, but I was absolutely ecstatic. Unfortunately, the back nine didn't work out quite as well. But for nine holes, I was hanging right around par on the most famous course in the world and I was the happiest golfer you could imagine.

Another memorable situation I remember was in 1998. I was set to play down in a foursome at the Floridian with GE CEO Jack Welch, *Today Show* host Matt Lauer, and Miami Dolphins owner Wayne Huizenga. We were playing the Floridian, which is a private course Wayne built for himself. Matt called and asked if I would mind if another person joined, which seemed a little strange, because I'd never seen or even heard of a five-some. Then he told me that the fifth person was Greg Norman, who was a friend of his and who had never played the course and really wanted to. The funny thing was, I called Welch and Huizenga, and both of them tried to back out. They were say-ing that I don't need another person because of the fivesome, but the two of them were really acting like kids, because they didn't want to play with Norman. But they all wanted to play that course, so they all showed up.

We're on the course, but before we start playing, there is this huge negotiation about which tees we're going to use. Remem-ber, this is between people who are used to negotiating deals for millions. We finally resolve it, so that Norman is going to play the championship tees, the professional tees, and we're going to play the members' tees. There are five sets of tees there, so we're playing on the third set and he's playing on the fifth. So we finally tee off. Greg is playing fine and so is Jack. Now Jack is playing with Matt against myself, Huizenga, and Norman. Through the front nine, Welch is playing even par and so is Norman. After a while, we can all see its starting to irritate Greg, even though he's using the professional tees. As we play it out, Jack is below par. We get down to the 16th hole, Jack, who's a great putter, misses about a four-foot putt, which he would make 70 percent of the time. At that point, he was two or three under and he parred the 17th. On the 18th, he's got about a three and a half–foot putt, which he would make 80 percent of the time. But he missed that putt, too, so he got a 69. But Norman ends up with a 70. So Jack beat Greg Norman and my team won the match as well, so it was really a remarkable day of golf.

I don't play that often with Jack, but a lot of my favorite golf memories involve him. I've played with him twice when he shot 69. The joke is, the better his round is, the worse mine is. Before he had his heart attack, we were playing with a bunch of our G.E. board members down at Augusta. Now Jack will play golf until there's nobody left to play with, from sunrise to sunset and most people can't keep up. We're trying to get a plane to get out of there at five o'clock and he was playing right up until like four thirty, five o'clock, and complaining that his stomach was bothering him. And he never complains. He had been on a trip to India and he was convinced that he'd gotten some kind of food poisoning and yet he played and played. At the end, he was using a cart to get around, because he wanted to play like nine more holes in an hour. Within eight hours, he had his heart attack.

The other time for me on a golf course that was really memorable was about fifteen months later and I wasn't even playing, although I was walking the course. It was in Nantucket, where Jack was in the finals of the Sankaty Head Golf Club championship. He won the tournament, beating a lot of younger players, a little more than a year after he had the heart attack. It was really quite remarkable because he was walking, he didn't use a cart. That really stuck in my mind, because it was really, really tiring and he beat some extremely experienced players to win, so it was no fluke. It just goes to show what kind of horse that guy is and what golf can show you about a person's character.

Photo Credits

C. Michael Armstrong: Courtesy of C. Michael Armstrong

Miller Barber: Gary Newkirk/Getty Images

Bonnie Bernstein: CBS Sports

George Brett: Brian Bahr/Getty Images

George H. W. Bush: The George Bush Presidential Library

Billy Casper: © Bettmann/CORBIS

Frank Chirkinian: Courtesy of Frank Chirkinian

Roger Clemens: Harry How/Getty Images

Alice Cooper: Scott Halleran/Getty Images

Ben Crenshaw: Stephen Munday/Getty Images

Tom DeLay: Courtesy of Office of the House Majority Leader

Celine Dion: Courtesy of Celine Dion

Pete Dye: Ken May

Ken Eichele: Courtesy of Ken Eichele

Lee Elder: Courtesy of Lee Elder

Tom Fazio: © Tony Roberts/CORBIS

Tim Finchem: Harry How/Getty Images

Raymond Floyd: David Cannon/Getty Images

Bill Gadsby: Courtesy of Bill Gadsby

Larry Gatlin: Courtesy of Larry Gatlin

Rod Gilbert: New York Rangers/Bruce Bennett Studios

Bryant Gumbel: Steve Burton/Courtesy of AT&T Pebble Beach
    National Pro-Am

Bob Hope: Getty Images

Gordie Howe: Courtesy of Gordie Howe

Bruce Jenner: Stephen Dunn/Getty Images

Matt Lauer: Courtesy of Matt Lauer

David Leadbetter: Courtesy of David Leadbetter

Jack Lemmon: Gary Newkirk/Getty Images

Huey Lewis: Andy Lyons/Getty Images

Branford Marsalis: Josef Astor

Casey Martin: Andy Lyons/Getty Images

Mark McCormack: David Gamble

A. J. McLean: Scott Halleran/Getty Images

Meat Loaf: Jamie Squire/Getty Images

Jim Nantz: AT&T Cox Classic

Craig T. Nelson: Graig Jones/Getty Images

Chris O'Donnell: Courtesy of Chris O'Donnell

Arnold Palmer in 1953: © Bettmann/CORBIS

Arnold Palmer waving (cover): Stephen Munday/ Getty
   Images

Gary Player: Courtesy of Gary Player

Maury Povich: Courtesy of Maury Povich

Nick Price: Stephen Munday/ Getty Images

Dan Quayle: Stephen Dunn/Getty Images

Judy Rankin: David Cannon/Getty Images

Kenny Rogers: © Jason Szenes/CORBIS SYGMA

Justin Timberlake: Scott Halleran/Getty Images

Peter Ueberroth: Tom O'Neal/TGO, Courtesy of AT&T Pebble
   Beach National Pro-Am

Karrie Webb: Warren Little/Getty Images

Jack Welch: Timothy Greenfield-Sanders

Bob Wright: Courtesy of Bob Wright